Canadian Heritage Breads

Paré • Pirk • Darcy

Library and Archives Canada Cataloguing in Publication
Paré, Jean, author
Canadian heritage breads / Jean Paré, Wendy Pirk, James Darcy,.

(Original series)
Includes index.
ISBN 978-1-988133-03-4 (wire-o)

1. Bread. 2. Cooking (Bread). 3. Baking. 4. Cookbooks.
I. Pirk, Wendy, author II. Darcy, James, author III. Title.

TX769.P363 2016 641.81'5 C2015-903582-1

Thanks to Jessica Knight for her contributions to the recipes and the 'How to' photos in the introduction, Ashley Billey for her food styling and help with the recipes, Sandy Weatherall of Jinsei Photographics for her photography and to Jennifer Ogle for her contribution.

Distributed by
Canada Book Distributors
www.canadabookdistributors.com
www.companyscoming.com
Tel: 1-800-661-9017

We acknowledge the financial support of the Government of Canada.
Nous reconnaissons l'appui financier du gouvernement du Canada.

Funded by the Government of Canada | Financé par le gouvernement du Canada | Canada

PC: 38-2

Table of Contents

INTRODUCTION

Canada is a land that was largely shaped by immigrants. Our country prides itself on being one of the most multi-cultural nations in the world. Canadian society is a blend of the aboriginal peoples and the settlers and immigrants who had the courage to leave their homes and carve out a place for themselves in a new, sometimes demanding land.

While they couldn't always find the ingredients and spices for their traditional dishes, they could use Canadian wheat to recreate the distinctive breads of their homeland.

Bread is window into our shared and unique cultures. I have heard it said that every civilization eats some variety of bread, whether they make it from wheat, corn or lentils. Historically in many regions breadmaking was a community event in which everyone brought their dough to a communal oven, and the loaves were baked together. Individuals often identified their breads by the unique symbol they had scored into their dough before handing it over to the master baker. Just as every family had its own symbol, every culture has its own bread. Today, whether it be leavened or unleavened, bread is the most widely eaten food in the world.

Canadian Wheat

Canadian all-purpose flour is different from those created in the U.S. or the UK. When we use recipes from cookbooks produced abroad, we have to adjust the amount of water to make the recipes work for us. The recipes in this book have been created and tested with our Canadian flour in mind.

Canadian wheat is world renowned. From Africa and Japan to Europe and the Middle East, our wheat is in demand. Even many U.S. bread and pasta manufacturers prefer to buy Canadian wheat than use crops grown in their own country. Although we are only the sixth largest wheat producer, we are one of the two largest wheat exporters worldwide. So, what makes Canadian wheat so special? In a word, protein.

Canadian hard wheat (hard red winter, hard red spring and hard white spring) and durum wheat are prized for their high protein content. Depending on the type of wheat, protein content can range from 10 to 15 percent. Canadian all-purpose flour, which is a combination of hard and soft wheat, has a protein content of 13 percent, making it possible to use for breadmaking rather than the specialized bread flours required in other countries.

In large part, we can thank our climate and farming practices for the high quality and content of protein in our wheat. The timing and amount of rain, as well as the temperatures during the growing season help to determine protein content, as do soil nitrogen levels and the amount and timing of fertilizer applied. It's a giant balancing act that Canadian wheat farmers have finessed and perfected over the years. Canada's cold winters also help maintain the high quality of our wheat by killing off most of the insects that would contaminate it, reducing the need for pesticides in both the growing and storing stage.

The type of wheat that is grown is also of immense importance. In the early days of Canadian settlement, wheat did not perform well. Immigrants brought with them the wheat they were used to growing in their homelands, which were not well suited to Canada's cold winters and shorter growing season. It wasn't until the introduction of Red Fife that wheat production really took off. First grown in Ontario in the 1840s, Red Fife soon spread to the prairies and became the Canadian wheat. By the early 1900s Marquis, a wheat developed from Red Fife specifically for Canadian growing conditions, had supplanted Red Fife as the wheat of choice. Most of the varieties of wheat grown in Canada today can trace their genetic makeup back to Marquis or Red Fife.

INGREDIENTS

The building blocks of bread are simple; if you have flour and water you can make bread. Most breads also contain yeast and salt. Of course you can embellish your dough with other ingredients such as eggs, butter, dried fruit, nuts or cheese, but even with just the four basic ingredients, you can create a truly astounding loaf of bread.

However, successful bread making requires an understanding of each of the four basic ingredients and the role they play in the creation of the perfect loaf.

Flour

Although you can make bread with many different types of flour, the most common is wheat. In North America, six classes of wheat grown are grown: hard red winter, hard red spring, hard white winter, durum, soft white winter and soft white spring. The hard varieties of wheat are used primarily for breads, and the softer varieties are better for pastries. Most of the wheat grown in the prairies is hard red spring wheat. Spring wheat tends to have a higher protein content than winter wheat, but many artisan bakers argue that the protein in winter wheat is a higher quality.

Protein Content

To make bread, you need a flour with a protein content of between 10.5 and 13 percent. Bread flour generally sits between 11 and 13 percent; most all-purpose flour sits between 9.5 and 12 percent, though Canadian all-purpose flour has 13 percent; and cake flour ranges from 6 to 8 percent. That said, you can't judge a flour by its name; some all-purpose and cake flours have a higher protein content, some bread flours a lower one, depending on the manufacturer.

Higher protein flours make breads with a good crust and chewy crumb; lower protein flours are better for softer breads, biscuits, sweet breads and the like. All-purpose flour is a combination of hard and soft wheat and, with it's high protein content, as the name suggests, has been formulated to have the widest use. Canadian all-purpose flour is excellent for making bread and as such, most of the recipes in this book have been created with all-purpose flour in mind.

Storing Flour

Store all-purpose flour in an air-tight container or keep it in the original paper bag and wrap it tightly in a plastic bag. Flour that is left open to the air can absorb moisture from humid air or lose moisture to dry air.

Whole wheat and whole grain flours should be stored in the freezer unless they will be used up within three months because they contain oils that will go rancid. They can be frozen for up to one year.

Water

Although it is an essential ingredient in breadmaking, not too much need be said about water. Basically it must be in the correct proportion to bind to the flour and provide the gluten structure, and it must be the correct temperature for the yeast to function properly.

The mineral content of your water might also affect the outcome of your breadmaking efforts. Minerals feed the yeast, so with very soft water, the yeast may underperform, making your dough quite sticky. With hard water, the high mineral content tightens the gluten strands, making your dough tough. If you are concerned about the mineral content of your water, you can use bottled water. Don't use distilled water, though, because it has had all mineral content removed.

Salt

Salt has many functions in the making of bread. First, it adds flavour. Bread made without salt is really bland. Salt also strengthens the gluten, holding the strands together so that they can stretch without tearing, meaning your dough will be more elastic and will rise better. Salt also slows down the activity of the yeast, ensuring that there are some sugars left to brown the crust, and it acts as a preservative, retaining moisture so the bread stays fresh longer.

It doesn't really matter what kind of salt you use as long as you consider the size of the grain; you'll get a lot more regular table salt in a teaspoon than you will coarse or kosher salt. Adjust your recipe accordingly.

Yeast

Yeast is a microorganism whose role in nature is to ferment things. In breadmaking it makes dough rise. Yeast feeds on simple sugars and produces carbon dioxide and alcohol. The carbon dioxide gets caught in cells in the dough, causing them to inflate rather like a balloon. The alcohol evaporates during the baking process, also causing the dough rise. Yeast lives in the air around us, but in the mid-1880s we began to cultivate it, and today there are four types of bakers yeast to choose from.

Fresh Yeast

The original type of cultivated yeast, fresh yeast is no longer widely used and can be a bit more challenging to find. It comes in the form of a beige brick or "cake" and can be found in the refrigerator section of some specialty stores. It must be stored in the fridge and loses its efficacy within a few days of being opened. Mix it with water before adding it to a recipe.

Instant Yeast

Also called bread yeast or bread machine yeast, this variety can be added directly to the flour in the recipe. However, it should not come into contact with cold liquid, sugar, salt or fats, including eggs. Sugar and salt will draw moisture away from the yeast, affecting its performance, and fat will coat the yeast, making it hard to distribute.

If you don't have the type of commercial yeast your recipe calls for, you can sub in another type, but the amount will need to be adjusted. To substitute fresh yeast, use half the amount of active dry yeast or a quarter of the amount of instant yeast.

Active Dry Yeast

This type of yeast looks like little pellets. It comes in packages and has a long shelf life. Before you use active dry yeast it must be reactivated by mixing it with water. To get the best performance from the yeast, the water should be about 105°F (40°C), but yeast will respond in colder water as well. Temperatures above 140°F (60°C) will kill the yeast. Once combined with water, active dry yeast must stand for 5 to 10 minutes, until it looks foamy.

Wild yeast

Before the advent of commercial yeast, bakers relied on wild yeast to make their breads, and sourdough breads still use this strategy. A starter dough of flour and water is allowed sit out in the open so wild yeast can attach to it and start the fermentation process. The starter is then added to the other ingredients to form a dough.

Thousands of strains of yeast naturally occur in the air around us, and different strains inhabit different areas. As a result, a starter from one region will taste slightly different than one grown elsewhere.

QUICK SOURDOUGH STARTER

Water	1 cup	250 mL
All-purpose flour	1 cup	250 mL
Active dry yeast	1/2 tsp.	2 mL

The night before you plan to make your bread, mix all 3 ingredients together and set out on a countertop in a draft-free area, allowing starter time to develop. Remaining starter can be left on the counter for future use; it is best stored at 65 to 77°F (18 to 25°C). To strengthen and "feed" starter, add 1/4 cup (60 mL) water and 1/2 cup (125 mL) flour every second day.

Breads made with wild yeast require more time to make than breads made with commercial yeast because it takes longer to cultivate the yeast strain, and wild yeast is slower at making dough rise. But as any sourdough aficionado can tell you, breads that have been fermenting longer have better, more complex flavours.

THE BASIC STEPS

Making bread can seem like a daunting task, but it needn't be. Just follow the steps outlined below and you'll be on your way to creating loaves that will do you proud!

Mixing

There are two main ways to make bread: the direct method and the preferment method. With the direct method, all the ingredients are combined at one time to make the dough. This method results in a "straight dough," which produces a bread that stales quickly and is best eaten the same day as it is baked.

With the preferment method, the dough is made in two steps. First a starter is created by combining flour, water and commercial yeast. It is left for a specified length of time before being added to the remaining ingredients to form a dough. These breads usually have better texture and more depth of flavour, and they last longer than straight dough breads because the fermented dough contains acids that act as natural preservatives. Sourdough is a type of prefermented bread in which only the starter is made with wild rather than commercial yeast.

Autolyse

After the dough has come together, many bakers suggest letting it rest for a while before you begin kneading. This resting period is called autolyse. As the dough rests, biological and chemical processes going on in within it begin to strengthen the gluten structure, making the dough easier to work with.

Kneading

For the novice baker, kneading can be intimidating. Wheat flour has two proteins that, when they come into contact with water, bond to form gluten. Gluten is largely responsible for giving bread its structure. Kneading dough helps develop the gluten, and the more the dough is kneaded, the stronger and more elastic the gluten structure becomes. Kneading also adds oxygen to the dough, which the yeast needs to make the dough rise.

To check if you've kneaded your dough enough, do the "gluten windowpane test." Stretch a piece of dough until you can see through it. If the dough rips, it's not ready; if it stretches without tearing, it has been kneaded enough.

Kneading can be done by hand or with a stand mixer. To knead by hand, on a lightly floured surface with lightly floured hands, push the dough away from you, then fold the far end back over the top, rotate the dough and repeat, adding more flour as necessary.

A stand mixer does a great job kneading, just remember to keep the speed low, and watch that the dough doesn't overheat during a long kneading time, which could affect the yeast's performance.

Bulk Fermentation

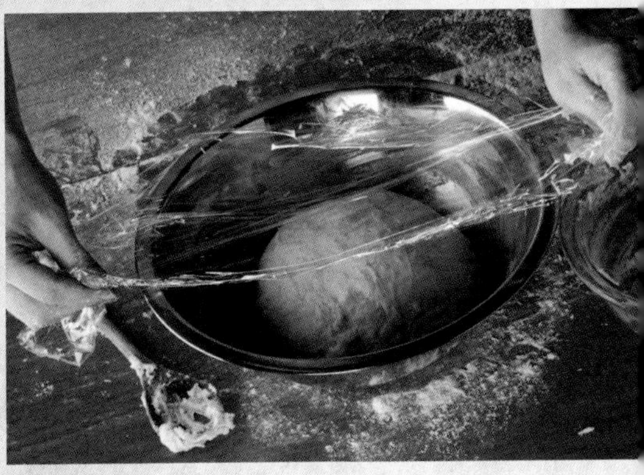

Once the dough has been kneaded, it must rise, a stage professional bakers call bulk fermentation. During this initial rise, the dough begins to develop its flavour and structure. Most recipes call for the dough to double in size during this stage. Letting the dough stand in the oven with the light on and door closed creates a perfect environment for the yeast to do its work. Be sure to cover the bowl with plastic wrap because the dough must retain its moisture to proof, and the plastic wrap traps the moisture in the bowl.

Deflating

After its initial rise, your dough needs to be deflated to release the gases that have built up and to reinvigorate the yeast. Although it is often called "punching down," you want to use a gentle touch when deflating your dough so as not to tear or damage the gluten structure. Sandwich breads and cinnamon rolls can be gently pushed in the centre to deflate. Other types of bread, like baguettes and dinner buns, do better if you simply fold the dough a few times onto itself during the bulk fermentation stage.

Shaping

When shaping the dough, do not overhandle it, and use a gentle touch, or you'll end up with dense bread.

Proofing

Proofing is the final rise the dough undergoes before baking. This step is essential for most breads to be sure they perform well in the oven. Underproofed bread will not rise to its full potential, and overproofed bread will collapse in the early stages of baking.

For most breads, the dough should rise until almost doubled in size, and it will slowly spring back when poked with a finger. Dough that has not proofed enough will spring back quickly, and dough that doesn't spring back has been overproofed.

Scoring

The final step before baking many types of breads is scoring the dough with a sharp knife or razor blade. Scoring not only improves the look of the final loaf, it also allows the crust to break where you want it to rather than bursting open randomly as the bread cooks. Controlling where the crust breaks ensures the bread rises evenly. Soft dough should not be scored too deeply or it will spread instead of rising.

Baking

As long as you've set your oven to the correct temperature, the baking step should go smoothly. Some breads require steam in the early stages of baking to ensure the surface of the dough stays soft enough to allow the dough to stretch to its full potential. Our favourite method is to spritz the inside of the oven every few minutes with a spray bottle. Make sure you don't spray the window, though, or you could crack the glass.

Cooling

Once your bread has been baked to perfection, transfer it to a cooling rack and sit back and admire your handiwork. Very few things in life can compete with the heaven that is freshly baked bread still warm from the oven, but don't reach for your serrated knife just yet. As bread cools, water molecules make their way from the interior to the crust, where they evaporate. If you cut into the loaf too soon, your bread will have a doughy crumb.

SCALING

Creativity in the kitchen is a great thing, and some of the best cooking is done by adding a little dash of this and a pinch of that, going by gut rather than a recipe. Not so with baking—particularly not breadmaking. Baking is precise, and recipes are formulas, ensuring that the correct ratio of ingredients are included so they can interact with each other as needed to produce the end product. Measurements need to be exact or the formula of the recipe will be thrown off and can yield disappointing results.

Professional bakers insist that all ingredients should be weighed rather than measured. Environmental conditions change, sometimes by the moment, and can have an enormous effect on the ingredients. A cup of flour in one kitchen might be more than a cup in a different kitchen, or even the same kitchen on a different day, depending on how much moisture the flour has absorbed from the surrounding air. By scaling, you can ensure that you are getting exactly the same amount of each ingredient every time.

Because this book is aimed at the home cook, we've kept it simple with the familiar measuring cups and spoons, but we've provided a conversion chart for some of the key ingredients, should you want to give scaling a try.

INGREDIENT	VOLUME	WEIGHT
Flour	1 cup / 250 mL	4.5 ounces / 128 grams
Table salt	1 teaspoon / 5 mL	0.25 ounces / 7 grams
Instant yeast	2 1/2 teaspoons / 12 mL	0.25 ounces / 7 grams
	1 teaspoon / 5 mL	0.11 ounces / 3 grams
Sugar	2 tablespoons / 30 mL	1 ounce / 28 grams
	1 1/2 teaspoons / 7 mL	0.25 ounces / 7 grams
Butter, oil, water, milk	1 cup / 250 mL	8 ounces / 227 grams
	2 tablespoons / 30 mL	1 ounce / 28 grams
Eggs	1 large egg	1.65 ounces / 47 grams
Dried fruit	2 1/3 cups / 575 mL	16 ounces / 454 grams
	1 cup / 250 mL	6 ounces / 170 grams
Nuts (coarsely chopped)	3 1/3 cups / 825 mL	16 ounces / 454 grams
	1 cup / 250 mL	4.8 ounces / 136 grams

Basic White Bread

Bread has been a staple of countless civilizations since time immemorial. Ever since people learned to thresh grain, they've been grinding it into flour and making it into some form of bread product. Until the late 1800s, most wheat breads were made out of whole wheat flour. The technology to separate the grain from the bran and the germ was unknown before that time. When white flour was introduced, it was too expensive for the majority of people; white bread was reserved for the well-to-do, and whole grain breads were considered peasant food. Funny, then, that today there has been a complete reversal in attitude, with white bread being seen as common and whole grain breads being more expensive and more highly regarded because of their nutritious ingredients. But let's be honest here. Sure, we all know that we should be eating whole grain bread, but nothing is more homey or comforting than a slice of fresh homemade white bread that is still warm from the oven.

Sugar	**1 tsp.**	**5 mL**
Warm water	**1/2 cup**	**125 mL**
1/4 oz. (7 g) package of active dry yeast	**1**	**1**
Sugar	**2 tbsp.**	**30 mL**
Butter (or hard margarine), softened	**2 tbsp.**	**30 mL**
Salt	**2 tsp.**	**10 mL**
Milk, scalded and cooled to lukewarm	**2 cups**	**500 mL**
All-purpose flour	**2 cups**	**500 mL**
All-purpose flour	**4 1/2 cups**	**1.1 L**

Stir first amount of sugar into warm water in a large bowl. Sprinkle yeast over top. Let stand 10 minutes. Stir to dissolve yeast.

Add remaining sugar, butter, salt, milk and first amount of flour. In a stand mixer, beat on low to moisten. Beat on high until smooth.

Work in enough remaining flour until dough pulls away from sides of bowl. Turn out onto a floured surface. Knead 8 to 10 minutes until smooth and elastic. Place in a greased bowl, turning once to grease top. Cover with a tea towel. Let stand in oven with light on and door closed for 1 to 1 1/2 hours until doubled in size. Punch dough down. Divide into 2 equal portions. Shape into loaves. Place in 2 greased 9 x 5 x 3 inch (23 x 12.5 x 7.5 cm) loaf pans. Cover with a tea towel. Let stand in oven with light on and door closed 35 to 45 minutes until doubled in size. Bake in 400°F (200°C) oven for about 30 minutes until browned. Loaves will sound hollow when tapped. Turn out onto racks to cool. Makes 2 loaves. Each loaf cuts into 18 slices.

1 slice: *100 Calories; 1 g Total Fat (0 g Mono, 0 g Poly, 0 g Sat); trace Cholesterol; 19 g Carbohydrate (trace Fibre, 2 g Sugar); 3 g Protein; 140 mg Sodium*

Yukon Sourdough

Before packaged yeast was readily available, breads were made with starters. The starters that originated in San Francisco were exceptionally sour thanks to the local strains of wild yeast (hence "sourdough"). Prospectors from the California gold rush carried the starters to the Yukon during the Klondike Gold Rush. They made sourdough breads, biscuits and pancakes, sometimes the only food available to them during the northern winter. Starters were so important that each prospector carried his in a pouch around his neck during the day and slept with it at night to keep it from freezing. Their legacy carries on, with people in the Klondike sharing the original sourdough starters. My family still keeps one alive.

Water	**7 tbsp.**	**100 mL**
Quick sourdough starter (see p. 9)	**1 cup**	**250 mL**
White bread flour	**1 1/2 cups**	**375 mL**
Water	**7 tbsp.**	**100 mL**
White bread flour	**1 1/2 cup**	**375 mL**
Whole wheat bread flour	**1/2 cup**	**125 mL**
Salt	**1 1/2 tsp.**	**7 mL**
Sugar	**1 tsp.**	**5 mL**
White bread flour	**1 tbsp.**	**15 mL**

Pour first amount of water into bread machine pan. Add starter. Sprinkle first amount of flour over top, covering liquid completely. Set machine to dough setting and start. Mix for 10 minutes, then turn machine off and let dough stand in machine for 8 hours.

Place remaining water into machine pan and sprinkle over second amount of white flour and whole wheat flour, covering liquid completely. Place salt and sugar in separate corners of machine pan. Set machine to dough setting and start.

When dough cycle has finished, transfer dough to a floured surface. Punch it down gently and shape into a ball. Place ball onto a lightly floured baking sheet and cover with a well-oiled piece of plastic wrap. Leave for approximately 2 hours or until doubled in size.

Dust loaf with remaining flour. Bake in 450°F (230°C) for 25 minutes, spraying oven three times with water in the first 5 minutes. Reduce temperature to 400°F (200°C) and bake loaf for 10 more minutes until golden and hollow-sounding when tapped on bottom. Tansfer to a wire rack to cool. Makes 1 loaf. Cut into 18 slices.

1 slice: *110 Calories; 0.5 g Total Fat (0 g Mono, 0 g Poly, 0 g Sat); 0 mg Cholesterol; 23 g Carbohydrate (1 g Fibre, 0 g Sugar); 4 g Protein; 200 mg Sodium*

Red Fife Flour Seed Bread

The Canadian prairies are known for a wonderful artisan whole grain bread called Red Fife, so called for the grain that was grown by early settlers in the area. Red Fife is the oldest variety of wheat named in Canada. Brought to Canada from Scotland and first grown in the 1840s in Otanabee, Ontario, by David Fife, it gradually replaced other varieties as it was resistant to rust. As it grew in popularity, it spread to the prairies and became the *Canadian wheat until around 1900, when it was bred with other varieties that were more resistant to pests and fungal growth. Red Fife might have been entirely forgotten had Sharon Rempel not replanted one pound of the seeds in 1988 and spread the subsequent seed harvest amongst growers and seed savers. Red Fife is now enjoying a resurgence in popularity as people become more interested in heritage grains, especially those that are grown locally and organically.*

All-purpose or bread flour	**2 cups**	**500 mL**
Red Fife flour	**2 cups**	**500 mL**
Muesli	**1/2 cup**	**125 mL**
Salt	**1 1/2 tsp.**	**7 mL**
Active dry yeast	**1/2 tsp.**	**2 mL**
Warm water	**2 1/4 cups**	**550 mL**
Vegetable oil	**2 tbsp.**	**30 mL**

In a large mixing bowl, combine both flours, muesli and salt. Stir in yeast and salt until evenly distributed.

Add water and stir until a soft dough forms. Cover bowl with plastic wrap and let stand in oven with light on and door closed for 12 to 14 hours, until doubled in size.

Turn dough out onto a flat surface and knock it down in centre. Knead for 8 to 10 minutes. Place it back in bowl and toss with oil until evenly coated. Shape into an oval loaf and place on a greased baking sheet. Let rest, uncovered, in oven with light on and door closed for 2 to 3 hours until doubled in size. Bake in 425°F (220°C) oven for 45 minutes. Transfer to a wire rack to cool. Makes 1 loaf. Cuts into 18 slices.

1 slice: *110 Calories; 0.5 g Total Fat (0 g Mono, 0 g Poly, 0 g Sat); 0 mg Cholesterol; 22 g Carbohydrate (2 g Fibre, trace Sugar); 4 g Protein; 200 mg Sodium*

Soldiers' Bread

This bread dates back to the 17th century when it was baked at the Fortress of Louisbourg in Nova Scotia as part of the soldiers' rations. Every soldier was allotted one 6-pound (2 .7 kg) loaf every four days, but no one wanted to eat 3- or 4-day-old bread, so the soldiers banded together. One soldier would collect his bread and share it with the group, then the next day another soldier would collect his bread and share it, and so on, so that the men ate fresh bread every day. This bread is still available from the bakery at the Fortress of Louisbourg National Historic Site, where they bake it in replicas of the traditional brick ovens. It is made from stone ground whole wheat and rye flour which gives it its dark colour, rich crumb and density. Although it was traditionally eaten with salt pork, nowadays most people enjoy it as an ideal sandwich bread.

Warm water	**6 cups**	**1.5 L**
Sugar	**1 tbsp.**	**15 mL**
Dry active yeast	**2 tbsp.**	**30 mL**
Rye flour	**4 cups**	**1 L**
Whole wheat flour	**3 cups**	**750 mL**
Salt	**2 tbsp.**	**30 mL**
Whole wheat flour	**9 cups**	**2.2 L**

Mix together water, sugar, yeast, rye flour and first amount of whole wheat flour. Beat until well combined, about 1 minute. Cover and let stand for 1 hour.

Mix in salt. Add remaining flour 1 cup (250 mL) at a time until a dough forms. Turn out onto a floured surface and knead for 15 minutes. Place in a greased bowl, turning once to grease top. Cover and let stand in oven with light on and door closed for about 1 hour until doubled in size. Punch dough down and knead for 5 minutes. Divide into 4 equal portions and shape into slightly flattened rounds. Place on greased baking sheets 4 inches (10 cm) apart. Let stand in oven with light on and door closed for 45 minutes. Bake in 400°F (200°C) oven for 20 minutes. Reduce heat to 350°F (175°C) and bake for 45 minutes. Turn out onto wire racks to cool. Makes 4 loaves. Each loaf cuts into 12 slices.

1 slice: *140 Calories; 1 g Total Fat (0 g Mono, 0 g Poly, 0 g Sat); 0 mg Cholesterol; 30 g Carbohydrate (5 g Fibre, 0 g Sugar); 6 g Protein; 730 mg Sodium*

Red River Bread

Red River cereal is a Canadian brand of hot cereal that originated in Manitoba's Red River Valley in 1924. It is a mix of cracked wheat, rye and flax and is known for its nutty flavour. The cereal gives this wholesome bread a lightness not usually found in whole wheat breads. Red River bread also has a nice soft crumb, ideal for building the perfect sandwich. You have to plan ahead when making this bread because the sponge needs to sit for at least 12 hours before it is ready to use.

Red River cereal	**1 cup**	**250 mL**
Whole wheat flour	**1 1/4 cups**	**275 mL**
Lukewarm water	**1 1/4 cups**	**275 mL**
Instant yeast	**1/4 tsp.**	**1 mL**
Lukewarm water	**1 3/4 cups**	**425 mL**
Whole wheat flour	**2 cups**	**500 mL**
Butter, melted	**3 tbsp.**	**45 mL**
Honey	**1/4 cup**	**60 mL**
Salt	**1 1/2 tsp.**	**7 mL**
Instant yeast	**1 tbsp.**	**15 mL**
Bread flour	**2 1/2 cups**	**625 mL**

Combine Red River cereal and first amounts of whole wheat flour, lukewarm water and yeast in a medium bowl to form a sponge. Cover with plastic wrap and let stand 12 to 15 hours.

Place sponge in a large bowl and add remaining lukewarm water. Stir until sponge dissolves. Add remaining whole wheat flour and mix well. Stir in butter and honey. Stir in salt. Stir in remaining yeast.

Add enough bread flour so that dough does not stick to sides of bowl. On a floured surface, knead dough 8 to 10 minutes until soft and elastic. Place in a greased bowl and cover with plastic wrap. Let stand in oven with light on and door closed for 1 hour, until doubled in size. Remove dough from bowl and divide into two pieces. Shape into loaves and put in greased 9 x 5 x 3 inch (23 x 12.5 cm x 7.5) bread pans. Cover tightly with plastic wrap. Let stand in oven with light on and door closed for about 40 minutes until doubled in size. Bake in 375°F (190°C) oven for 30 to 40 minutes. Transfer to a wire rack to cool. Makes 2 loaves. Each loaf cuts into 18 slices.

***1 slice:** 100 Calories; 1.5 g Total Fat (0 g Mono, 0 g Poly, 0.5 g Sat); trace Cholesterol; 20 g Carbohydrate (2 g Fibre, 2 g Sugar); 3 g Protein; 100 mg Sodium*

Pumpernickel

No one seems to agree why it was named "pumpernickel," but historical sources reveal that this bread originated in the Westphalia region of Germany, where it was already being baked in the mid 15th century. Originally "peasant fare," pumpernickel bread has recently gained popularity thanks to its nutritious ingredients and its prominence in delis throughout Europe and North America. It is the best known of Germany's kastenbrots, *or "box breads" and was traditionally steam-baked for about 20 hours in a lidded pan (hence the "box bread" title), giving the bread its characteristic dense, moist, chewy texture and slightly sour taste. Because most of us do not have that much time to dedicate to breadmaking, we've shortened the process in this recipe, with delicious results.*

Rye flour	**4 cups**	**1 L**
Whole wheat flour	**2 cups**	**500 mL**
Bulgur wheat	**2/3 cup**	**150 mL**
Salt	**2 tsp.**	**10 mL**
Molasses	**2 tbsp.**	**30 mL**
Warm water	**3 1/2 cups**	**1.6 kg**
Vegetable oil	**1 tbsp.**	**15 mL**

Combine both flours, bulgur and salt in a large bowl.

In a small bowl, stir molasses into warm water. Add to flour mixture. Stir in oil until dough comes together. Divide dough into 2 greased 9 x 5 x 3 inch (23 x 12.5 x 7.5 cm) loaf pans, making sure to press it all the way into corners of pans. Cover with greased plastic wrap and let stand in oven with light on and door closed for 18 to 24 hours. Remove plastic wrap and cover pans with foil. Fill a roasting pan with boiling water and place a rack over top. Place pans on rack and bake in 225°F (110°C) oven for 4 hours. Remove foil and bake in 325°F (160°C) oven for 30 to 40 minutes, adding water to roasting pan if necessary, until loaves are firm and top is crusty. Let stand for 5 minutes before transfering to a wire rack to cool. Makes 2 loaves. Each loaf cuts into 16 slices.

1 slice: *90 Calories; 1 g Total Fat (0 g Mono, 0 g Poly, 0 g Sat); 0 mg Cholesterol; 19 g Carbohydrate (4 g Fibre, 1 g Sugar); 4 g Protein; 150 mg Sodium*

Black Bread

Traditionally most families in Russia made their breads with rye flour, which was cheaper and more nutritious than wheat flour; white bread was reserved for the more affluent members of society. Black bread was a staple and was seen as a symbol of good health and also of hardship because it was sometimes one of the only things that kept people from starving. Pieces were usually torn off the loaf instead of sliced, and were often served with soups. There is no standard black bread recipe because every family had its own version. In the past, this bread would have been made with a sourdough starter that was cultivated over a few days, but we've skipped that step and used yeast instead.

Rye flour	**3 1/2 cups**	**875 mL**
All bran cereal (100% bran)	**3/4 cup**	**175 mL**
Cocoa	**1/4 cup**	**60 mL**
Salt	**2 tsp.**	**10 mL**
Caraway seeds (optional)	**1 tsp.**	**5 mL**
Butter (or hard margarine), softened	**1/4 cup**	**60 mL**
Instant coffee granules	**1 tbsp.**	**15 mL**
Cooking molasses	**1/3 cup**	**75 mL**
Fennel seeds	**1/2 tsp.**	**2 mL**
Onion powder	**1 tsp.**	**5 mL**
Water	**2 1/4 cups**	**550 mL**
Sugar	**1 tsp.**	**5 mL**
Warm water	**1/4 cup**	**60 mL**
1/4 oz. (7 g) packages active dry yeast	**2**	**2**
All-purpose flour	**3 1/2 cups**	**875 mL**

Measure first 10 ingredients into a large bowl. Add water. Beat on low to moisten.

In a small bowl, stir sugar into warm water. Sprinkle yeast over top. Let stand 10 minutes. Stir to dissolve yeast. Add to contents in large bowl. Beat on low to moisten. Beat on high until smooth.

Work in enough all-purpose flour so dough pulls away from sides of bowl. Turn out onto a floured surface. Knead 8 to 10 minutes until smooth and elastic. Place in a greased bowl, turning once to grease top. Cover with a tea towel. Let stand in oven with light on and door closed for 45 to 60 minutes until dough is almost doubled in size. Punch dough down.

(continued on next page)

Divide into 2 equal portions. Shape into round loaves and put in 2 greased 8 inch (20 cm) round cake layer pans. Flatten slightly. Cover with a tea towel. Let stand in oven with light on and door closed for 30 to 45 minutes until almost doubled in size. Slash tops of loaves with a sharp knife. Make about 3 slashes per loaf. Bake in 375°F (190°C) oven for 35 to 40 minutes. Loaves should sound hollow when tapped. Turn out onto racks to cool. Makes 2 loaves. Each loaf cuts into 18 slices.

***1 slice:** 110 Calories; 2 g Total Fat (0 g Mono, 0 g Poly, 1 g Sat); trace Cholesterol; 21 g Carbohydrate (3 g Fibre, 2 g Sugar); 3 g Protein; 135 mg Sodium*

Why They Came...the French

Although they were not the first to arrive in Canada, the French were the first Europeans to settle permanently here. By the time Jacques Cartier landed in 1534 and claimed the Gaspé Peninsula for the King of France, the British had already claimed part of the east coast, and Spanish, Portuguese and Basque ships were fishing off the coast of Newfoundland. Cartier had come to Canada in search of a northwest passage to India and valuable minerals, particularly gold, and when he found neither, he and the French monarchy set their sights on other lands. They basically lost interest in what would become Canada until 1605, when their first settlement in Canada, Port-Royal, was built in what was then Acadia but is now Nova Scotia. In 1608, Samuel de Champlain, sent to New France to explore and map the territory, founded what is now Québec City. Although Champlain tried to convince France to take a greater interest the colony, the monarchy did not see New France as a priority and did little to establish a stronger French presence here.

Many of the early French explorers that journeyed to New France were drawn by the fur trade. They became *coureurs de bois,* literally "runners of the woods," and traded with the Indigenous peoples, bringing them European goods in exchange for their animal pelts. *Coureurs des bois* were indispensable to the early settlements in New France because they learned the customs of the local people and brought these skills to the French settlers, helping them cope in the wilderness of an unfamiliar land. *Coureurs des bois* worked for themselves, and as the fur trade continued to grow, they were regarded as little more than outlaws by the licenced fur-trading companies, who resented the competition. *Voyageurs,* on the other hand, were explorers hired by the licenced traders to man their canoes as they sought lucrative fur-trading opportunities.

Québec City became the capital of New France and the main port of trade, but the colony's population remained low, giving France a much smaller presence in the New World than the British, who were also heavily involved in the fur trade. To help increase the population, in the mid 1660s, the King of France sent about 800 young women to New France. These women, known as *Les Filles du Roi* (the King's Daughters), were meant to marry French colonists and start families.

Settlers in New France, known as *les habitants,* were mostly Catholic and lived according to the customs of France.

The relationship between France and England was strained both in Europe and in their colonies in the New World. Both battled for supremacy in the fur trade, as well as for a bigger slice of the continent that supplied that trade. In 1755, British soldiers began pushing the Acadians off their land because the Acadians refused to swear allegiance to the British Crown. Many of these Acadians returned to France, while others resettled in Louisiana, where they became known as the Cajuns.

In 1759, after the Battle of the Plains of Abraham at Québec City, New France fell under British control. Although they were now subjects of the British monarchy, French settlers refused to bend to British rule. They maintained their language and customs, and their culture is still alive and well in Canada today.

Baguette

Today many bakers in France still rise before dawn to make those special long loaves of bread we know as baguettes. They still bake the bread in the time-honoured way—first in a steamy, moist atmosphere and then in dry heat to crisp the crust—that makes French loaves like no other. Because of this special baking process and the particular type of flour used in France, it is difficult for the home baker in Canada to produce an authentic baguette, but this recipe yields impressive results that are much tastier than many commercially prepared loaves.

All-purpose flour	**2 cups**	**500 mL**
Salt	**2 tsp.**	**10 mL**
1/4 oz. (7 g) packages active dry yeast	**2**	**2**
Sugar	**1 tbsp.**	**15 mL**
Warm water	**2 cups**	**500 mL**
All-purpose flour	**3 cups**	**750 mL**
Cornmeal, sprinkle		

Combine first amount of flour, salt, yeast and sugar in a large bowl. Add warm water. Beat on low to moisten. Beat on high for 3 minutes.

Work in enough remaining flour until dough pulls away from sides of bowl. Turn out onto a floured surface. Knead 8 to 10 minutes until smooth and elastic. Place in a greased bowl, turning once to grease top. Cover with a tea towel. Let stand in oven with light on and door closed for 1 to 1 1/4 hours until doubled in size. Punch dough down. Divide into 2 equal portions.

On a floured surface, roll each portion into a long, narrow loaf, up to the length your oven will hold. Place on a greased baking sheet that has been sprinkled with cornmeal. Cover with a tea towel. Let stand in oven with light on and door closed for about 45 minutes until almost doubled in size. Make 3 diagonal cuts 1/8 inch (3 mm) deep across top of each loaf. Bake in 375°F (190°C) oven for 30 to 35 minutes. Turn out onto racks to cool. Makes 2 loaves. Each loaf cuts into 24 slices.

2 slices: *160 Calories; 0 g Total Fat (0 g Mono, 0 g Poly, 0 g Sat); 0 mg Cholesterol; 33 g Carbohydrate (1 g Fibre, trace Sugar); 5 g Protein; 200 mg Sodium*

Oatmeal Bread

Early settlers from Europe first brought oats to Canada; they were one of the easiest crops to grow and were a good match for the soils. Then, as today, oats were mostly used for animal feed, but settlers also made them into cereals, oatcakes and breads. By themselves, oats do not make good bread and would have been mixed with wheat to give the bread better structure, and to help stretch out the more expensive wheat flour supply so it would last longer. Today, the lowly oat is enjoying an upsurge in popularity as health-conscious consumers seek loaves that contain more nutritious ingredients. Artisan bakery and even supermarket shelves are now stocked with all manner of oat breads.

Rolled oats	**1 cups**	**250 mL**
Butter (or hard margarine)	**3 tbsp.**	**45 mL**
Fancy molasses	**1/4 cup**	**60 mL**
Boiling water	**2 cups**	**500 mL**
Warm water	**1/4 cup**	**60 mL**
Sugar	**1 tsp.**	**5 mL**
1/4 oz. (7 g) package of active dry yeast	**1**	**1**
Brown sugar, packed	**1/3 cup**	**75 mL**
Salt	**2 tsp.**	**10 mL**
All-purpose flour	**2 cups**	**500 mL**
All-purpose flour	**4 cups**	**1 L**
Large egg white	**1**	**1**
Water	**1 tbsp.**	**15 mL**
Rolled oats	**1/4 cup**	**60 mL**

Combine first amount of rolled oats, butter and molasses in a large bowl. Stir in boiling water and set aside to cool to lukewarm.

Combine warm water and sugar in a small bowl. Sprinkle yeast over top. Let stand 10 minutes. Stir to dissolve yeast. Add to warm rolled oat mixture.

Add brown sugar, salt and first amount of flour. Beat well.

Work in enough remaining flour until dough pulls away from sides of bowl. Turn out onto a floured surface. Knead 8 to 10 minutes until smooth and elastic. Place in a greased bowl, turning once to grease top. Cover with a tea towel. Let stand in oven with light on and door closed for 1 to 1 1/2 hours until doubled in size. Punch dough down. Divide into 2 equal portions. Shape into loaves. Place in 2 greased 9 x 5 x 3 inch (23 x 12.5 x 7.5 cm) loaf pans. Cover with a tea towel. Let stand in oven with light on and door closed 20 to 40 minutes until doubled in size.

(continued on next page)

For the topping, beat egg white and water with a fork in a small bowl. Brush over tops of loaves. Sprinkle with remaining rolled oats. Bake in 350°F (175°C) oven for 45 to 50 minutes. Turn out onto racks to cool. Makes 2 loaves. Each loaf cuts into 18 slices.

1 slice: *110 Calories; 1.5 g Total Fat (0 g Mono, 0 g Poly, 0.5 g Sat); trace Cholesterol; 22 g Carbohydrate (trace Fibre, 4 g Sugar); 3 g Protein; 135 mg Sodium*

Raisin Bread

Different civilizations have been preserving fresh fruit by drying it in the sun since time immemorial. Writings by the ancient Egyptians describe their raisin-making process, the Romans used raisins as a form of barter currency, and Hannibal and his army snacked on raisins as they crossed the Alps, elephants in tow. It is impossible to say who first thought to add raisins to bread (though the U.S. credits beloved environmental writer Henry David Thoreau). People around the world have been tossing raisins into dough since at least the late 1600s, way before Thoreau baked his first loaf. However, because most of the raisins we eat in Canada are produced in California, we've chosen an American raisin bread recipe for this book. For best results, the raisins should be soft.

Milk	**1 1/4 cups**	**300 mL**
Butter (or hard margarine)	**1/2 cup**	**125 mL**
Sugar	**1/2 cup**	**125 mL**
Salt	**2 tsp.**	**10 mL**
Ground cinnamon	**2 tsp.**	**10 mL**
Sugar	**2 tsp.**	**10 mL**
Warm water	**1/2 cup**	**125 mL**
1/4 oz. (7 g) packages active dry yeast	**2**	**2**
Large eggs, beaten	**3**	**3**
All-purpose flour	**3 1/2 cups**	**875 mL**
Raisins	**2 cups**	**500 mL**
All-purpose flour	**3 1/2 cups**	**875 mL**
Butter	**2 tsp.**	**10 mL**

Scald milk in a saucepan. Remove from heat. Stir in first amounts of butter and sugar, salt and cinnamon. Stir to melt butter and dissolve sugar. Pour into a large bowl.

Stir remaining sugar into warm water in a small bowl. Sprinkle yeast over top. Let stand 10 minutes. Stir to dissolve yeast. Add to butter mixture.

Add eggs and first amount of flour. Beat on low to moisten. Beat on medium until smooth.

Stir in raisins. Work in enough remaining flour until dough pulls away from sides of bowl. Turn out onto a floured surface. Knead 8 to 10 minutes until smooth and elastic. Dough may seem a bit sticky but handles well with greased hands. Place in a greased bowl, turning once to grease top. Cover with a tea towel. Let stand in oven with light on and door closed for about 1 1/4 hours until doubled in size. Punch dough down. Divide in half. Shape into loaves. Place in 2 greased 9 x 5 x 3 inch (23 x 12.5 x 7.5 cm) loaf pans.

(continued on next page)

Cover with a tea towel. Let stand in oven with light on and door closed for about 45 minutes until doubled in size. Bake in 350°F (175°C) oven for about 35 minutes. Turn out onto racks to cool. Brush warm tops with remaining butter. Makes 2 loaves. Each loaf cuts into 18 slices.

1 slice: *160 Calories; 3.5 g Total Fat (1 g Mono, 0 g Poly, 2 g Sat); 25 mg Cholesterol; 29 g Carbohydrate (1 g Fibre, 10 g Sugar); 4 g Protein; 140 mg Sodium*

Ciabatta

You mat be surprised to hear that ciabatta is not a traditional Italian bread. It certainly looks like the type of hearty, rustic loaf that would have graced tables across the Italian countryside throughout the ages, but in truth, it was created in the 1980s by a baker/miller from a small town near Venice. At the time, the French baguette was sweeping the Italian market as a popular sandwich bread. In response, Arnaldo Cavallari set out to create a modern bread with traditional Italian character that could hold its ground against the baguette. He named his creation ciabatta, *the Italian word for "slipper," which he thought the bread resembled. It has become a staple in bakeries throughout Canada. The dough is very wet, which gives the bread its characteristic holey texture, but also means that it needs a longer rising time than most other leavened breads.*

Water	**7/8 cup**	**200 mL**
White bread flour	**1 1/2 cups**	**375 mL**
Instant yeast	**1/2 tsp.**	**2 mL**

Water	**7/8 cup**	**200 mL**
Milk	**2 tbsp.**	**30 mL**
Extra virgin olive oil	**2 tbsp.**	**30 mL**
White bread flour	**3 cups**	**750 mL**
Instant yeast	**1/4 tsp.**	**1 mL**
Salt	**1 1/2 tsp.**	**7 mL**
Granulated sugar	**1/2 tsp.**	**2 mL**

Add first amount of water to bread machine pan and sprinkle over first amount of flour. Make a dent in centre of flour and add first amount of yeast. Start bread machine on dough setting and mix for 5 minutes. Transfer dough to a large mixing bowl, cover with greased plastic wrap and let stand for at least 12 hours.

Return dough to pan and add remaining water, milk and oil. Sprinkle remaining flour over top. Make a dent in centre of flour and add remaining yeast. Add salt and sugar in separate corners of pan. Start bread machine on dough setting. When cycle is finished, transfer dough to a large bowl, cover with greased plastic wrap and let stand in oven with light on and door closed until tripled in size, about 1 hour. Divide dough in half and place each portion on a lightly floured baking sheet. Shape each portion into a long, 1 inch (2.5 cm) thick loaf. Sprinkle flour over each loaf and let stand, uncovered, in oven with light on and door closed for about 25 minutes, until dough has risen and spread. Bake in 425°F (220°C) oven for about 25 minutes, until loaves are golden and sound hollow when tapped. Transfer to wire racks to cool. Makes 2 loaves. Each loaf cuts into 12 slices.

1 slice: *105 Calories; 1.5 g Total Fat (1 g Mono, 0 g Poly, 0 g Sat); 0 mg Cholesterol; 19 g Carbohydrate (trace Fibre, 0 g Sugar); 3 g Protein; 150 mg Sodium*

Potato Bread

Potatoes became a staple in northern Europe in the mid 1700s, proving to be more reliable than many of the grain crops. For early settlers in the prairies, potatoes were a godsend; they took well to prairie soils and staved off starvation for many a family when other crops grew poorly. Polish peasants mixed mashed potatoes with rye or wheat flour, creating a bread that would rise higher than flour breads, thanks to the starch in the potato, and have a moist crumb. This recipe's roots can be traced back to Galicia, formerly a province in the Austro-Hungarian empire that is now the southeastern part of Poland.

Lukewarm water	**1/4 cup**	**60 mL**
1/4 oz. (7 g) package of active dry yeast	**1**	**1**
Sugar	**1 tsp.**	**5 mL**
Oil	**2 tbsp.**	**30 mL**
Large onion, chopped	**1**	**1**
All-purpose flour	**10 cups**	**2.5 L**
Salt	**1 tsp.**	**5 mL**
Pepper	**1/2 tsp.**	**2 mL**
Large potatoes	**6**	**6**
Eggs, lightly beaten	**3**	**3**

Pour water into a small cup or bowl. Stir in yeast and sugar and set aside, covered, until mixture foams, about 20 minutes.

Heat oil in a frying pan over medium. Add onion and sauté for about 5 minutes until it is transparent. Set aside to cool.

Combine flour, salt and pepper in a large mixing bowl. Peel and grate potatoes, setting aside any liquid. Add potatoes and potato liquid to the flour right away, before the potatoes start to blacken.

Add yeast mixture, eggs and fried onion, and mix it into a smooth dough. On a well-floured board, knead dough until it is no longer sticky, about 10 minutes. Place into a greased bowl and cover with plastic wrap. Let stand in oven with light on and door closed for about 2 hours, until doubled in size.

Shape dough into 2 round loaves. Let stand in oven with light on and door closed for about 45 minutes until doubled in size. Bake in 375°F (190°C) oven for 45 minutes, or until golden brown. Serve warm. Makes 2 loaves. Each loaf cuts into 18 slices.

***1 slice:** 90 Calories; 1.5 g Total Fat (0.5 g Mono, 0 g Poly, 0 g Sat); 20 mg Cholesterol; 17 g Carbohydrate (1 g Fibre, trace Sugar); 3 g Protein; 75 mg Sodium*

Icelandic Brown Bread

The Iceland Festival, which is celebrated on August 2 by Canadian Icelanders, marks the occasion when Icelandic immigrants first established a colony at Gimli, Manitoba, in 1875. Between 1870 and 1900, 25 percent of Icelanders left their country for the promise of a better life, many of them choosing "New Iceland" in Manitoba because of the availability of land and the similarity in climate. Canada now boasts one of the largest communities of ethnic Icelanders outside Iceland who primarily speak their native language and who have held fast to their traditions, including this dense, healthy, flavourful bread.

Active dry yeast	**2 tbsp.**	**30 mL**
Warm water	**1/4 cup**	**60 mL**
Very warm water	**2 1/2 cups**	**625 mL**
Honey	**1/4 cup**	**60 mL**
Cold-pressed canola oil	**1/2 cup**	**125 mL**
Blackstrap molasses	**1/2 cup**	**125 mL**
Whole wheat flour	**3 cups**	**750 mL**
All-purpose flour	**3 cups**	**750 mL**
Sea salt	**2 tsp.**	**10 mL**
Mix of your favourite nuts and seeds	**1 1/2 cups**	**375 mL**

In a small bowl, activate yeast with warm water and set aside for 5 to 10 minutes.

In a separate bowl, mix together very warm water, honey, oil and molasses. Cool to lukewarm.

In a third bowl, combine both flours and salt.

Stir yeast water into honey mixture. Stir in flour mixture 1 cup (250 mL) at a time. Add in nuts and seeds with last of flour. Turn dough out onto a lightly floured surface and knead for about 10 minutes, adding more flour, if necessary, to make it smooth. Place dough in an oiled bowl, turning once to coat top. Place in oven with light on and door closed until doubled in size, about 1 hour. Punch dough down and let rise again until doubled, about 20 to 30 minutes. Divide dough in half and place into 2 lightly oiled 9 x 5 x 3 inch (23 x 12.5 x 7.5 cm) loaf pans.

(continued on next page)

Let stand, covered, in oven with light on and door closed until each loaf rises to edge of pan. Bake in 400°F (200°C) oven for 15 minutes, then turn heat to 350°F (175°C) and bake until cooked, about 40 minutes. Transfer to wire racks to cool. Makes 2 loaves. Each loaf cuts into 18 slices.

1 slice: *150 Calories; 6 g Total Fat (2.5 g Mono, 2.5 g Poly, 0.5 g Sat); 0 mg Cholesterol; 21 g Carbohydrate (2 g Fibre, 4 g Sugar); 4 g Protein; 130 mg Sodium*

Pane Toscano

Most bakers would tell you that salt is an essential ingredient in bread, reinforcing the structure of the dough and enhancing the flavour, but centuries ago in Tuscany, breadmakers created a saltless loaf that has become the signature bread of the region. Tuscan lore has it that in the 1500s, people of the region disapproved of a salt tax that was instituted and chose instead to simply do without salt. The resulting bread, called "pane sciocco" (bread without salt) in Tuscany and "pane Toscano" throughout the rest of Italy, is a rather bland, dry bread that pairs perfectly with salty foods such as olives, anchovies, cured meats and cheeses. Traditionally it would have been baked in a wood-burning oven, and bread purists still swear by this method. You'll need to make the starter a day in advance.

White bread flour	**1 1/2 cups**	**375 mL**
Boiling water	**1 1/2 cups**	**375 mL**
Lukewarm water	**4 tbsp.**	**60 mL**
1/4 oz. (7 g) package of active dry yeast	**1**	**1**
White bread flour	**3 1/2 cups**	**875 mL**

To make the starter, combine first amount of flour with boiling water. Cover with a damp tea towel and let stand for 10 to 12 hours.

Sprinkle yeast into lukewarm water. Let stand 10 minutes. Stir to dissolve yeast. Add to starter.

Add remaining flour and mix to form a medium-soft dough. Turn out onto a lightly floured surface and knead until smooth and elastic, about 6 minutes. Place in a greased bowl, turning once to grease top, and cover with greased plastic wrap. Let stand in oven with light on and door closed until doubled in size, about 1 1/2 hours. Punch down and shape into a round loaf. With well-floured hands, fold sides of round into centre and seal. Shape into an oval.

Place on a lightly floured baking sheet, cover with greased plastic wrap and let stand in oven with light on and door closed until doubled in size, about 40 minutes. Punch down to about half its size, flip dough and cover with an upside down bowl. Let stand in oven with light on and door closed for about 30 minutes. Bake in 425°F (220°C) oven for 30 to 35 minutes until golden. Transfer to a wire rack to cool. Makes 1 loaf. Cuts into 16 slices.

***1 slice:** 160 Calories; 0.5 g Total Fat (0 g Mono, 0 g Poly, 0 g Sat); 0 mg Cholesterol; 31 g Carbohydrate (1 g Fibre, 0 g Sugar); 5 g Protein; 0 mg Sodium*

Brioche

This soft yeast bread enriched with loads of butter and eggs originated in France, where it rivals the croissant as a favourite breakfast food. It has not caught on quite as much in North America, but its popularity is on the rise, as is evidenced by the fact that high-end hamburger chains are swapping out the traditional hamburger bun in favour of brioche buns. This rich bread has as much (and sometimes more) butter as most pastries, but it is only slightly sweet. A stand mixer makes easier work of this recipe because it can be difficult to incorporate all the butter into the dough by hand.

Sugar	**1 tsp.**	**5 mL**
Warm water	**1/4 cup**	**60 mL**
1/4 oz. (7 g) package of active dry yeast	**1**	**1**
Butter (or hard margarine), softened	**1/2 cup**	**125 mL**
Sugar	**1/3 cup**	**75 mL**
Large eggs	**4**	**4**
Salt	**3/4 tsp.**	**4 mL**
All-purpose flour	**2 1/2 cups**	**625 mL**
Milk, scalded and cooled to lukewarm	**3/4 cup**	**175 mL**
All-purpose flour	**2 3/4 cups**	**675 mL**
Sugar	**1 tbsp.**	**15 mL**

Stir first amount of sugar in warm water in a small bowl. Sprinkle yeast over top. Let stand 10 minutes. Stir to dissolve yeast.

(continued on next page)

Cream butter and second amount of sugar in a large bowl. Separate 1 egg into yolk and white. Set white aside. Beat in remaining 3 eggs and extra egg yolk, 1 at a time.

Add salt, first amount of flour and yeast mixture. Beat on high until smooth.

Add milk and mix. Work in enough remaining flour so that dough pulls away from sides of bowl. Turn out onto a floured surface. Knead 8 to 10 minutes until smooth and elastic. Place in a greased bowl, turning once to grease top. Cover with a tea towel. Let stand in oven with light on and door closed for about 2 hours until doubled in size. Punch dough down. Divide into 3 equal portions. Cut and shape each portion into 8 buns and put into greased brioche bun cups or muffin cups. Cover with a tea towel. Let stand in oven with light on and door closed for about 1 hour until doubled in size.

Beat egg white and remaining sugar together. Brush tops of buns. Bake in 375°F (190°C) oven for about 15 minutes. Makes 24 buns.

***1 bun:** 70 Calories; 4.5 g Total Fat (1.5 g Mono, 0 g Poly, 2.5 g Sat); 45 mg Cholesterol; 5 g Carbohydrate (0 g Fibre, 4 g Sugar); 2 g Protein; 90 mg Sodium*

Why They Came...the Americans

With the longest undefended border in the world, it is no wonder that Canada and the United States have a lot in common. There is a great deal of similarity between our two cultures thanks largely to our proximity, shared language and commonality of social norms and values. A fair amount of immigration between the two nations occurs, and though today most of the movement is from Canada to the U.S., historically the flow was reversed.

The first significant wave of immigrants coming from our neighbours to the south began during the American Revolution, from 1775 to 1783. At the time the American public was bitterly divided. The Patriots, who were fed up with living under British rule, demanded the freedom to govern themselves, and the Loyalists, who were loyal to the British Crown, wanted to remain a British colony. At war's end, the Patriots stood victorious and saw the Loyalists as traitors. Patriots drove many Loyalists from their homes, and others fled north for fear of Patriot retribution. Still others relocated to Canada because they were unwilling to live in an America no longer under British rule. Most of these United Empire Loyalists settled in what is now Ontario, Québec and the Maritimes.

Canada also saw a fair amount of immigration from the U.S. during the days of slavery. During the War of 1812, American slaves were offered freedom in Canada if they were willing to fight on the side of the British. At least 2000 people accepted the offer. Afterwards, from the 1830s until the 1860s, Canada was a safe haven for escaped slaves. They were smuggled into the country via the Underground Railroad, where they could live free and out of the reach of their former task masters or bounty hunters who would return them to a life of enslavement. Because of its furtive nature, there is no way to know for sure how many people came to Canada by way of the Underground Railroad, but it has been suggested that the number may be as high as 100,000.

Gold fever also brought Americans onto what is now Canadian soil. The Fraser River Gold Rush in 1858 drew as many as 30,000 prospectors, many from the California Gold Rush, hoping the find their fortune. The influx of people into the area caused a lot of tension with local Indigenous people and prompted Britain to establish British Columbia as a colony, thereby maintaining sovereignty over the region. The Klondike Gold Rush, from 1897 to 1899, saw tens of thousands of people flock to the area, with most coming from the U.S. As a result, the Yukon territory was established and the area experienced unprecedented development, again at the expense of the local Indigenous people.

The last big wave of immigrants from the U.S. came in the years before 1914, when the Canadian government turned its focus to settling the prairies. More than 750,000 people, many of European descent who had originally moved to the American West, decided to head north and capitalize on the promise of free land for homesteaders.

Cheese Bread

It is near impossible to determine who deserves the credit for dreaming up cheese bread. At least as far back as Roman times people embellished their bread by adding cheese, and many nations have their own unique versions of cheese bread, using all different types of cheeses. The most common type of cheese bread in Canada, this version most likely originated in the U.S. and is made with Cheddar cheese. It can be found in many forms—loaves, sticks and buns, to name a few—in bakeries across the nation.

Milk	**1 1/2 cups**	**375 mL**
Grated sharp Cheddar cheese	**2 cups**	**500 mL**
Butter (or hard margarine), softened	**2 tbsp.**	**30 mL**
Sugar	**3 tbsp.**	**45 mL**
Sugar	**2 tsp.**	**10 mL**
Warm water	**1/2 cup**	**125 mL**
1/4 oz. (7 g) packages active dry yeast	**2**	**2**
Salt	**1 1/2 tsp.**	**7 mL**
All-purpose flour	**6 cups**	**1.5 L**

Scald milk in a medium saucepan. Remove from heat.

Stir in cheese and first amounts of butter and sugar. It is not a problem if cheese doesn't melt smooth. Cool to lukewarm.

Stir remaining sugar into warm water in a small bowl. Sprinkle yeast over top. Let stand 10 minutes. Stir to dissolve yeast. Add to cooled cheese mixture and mix well. Pour into a large bowl.

Combine salt and flour. Work in enough flour until dough pulls away from sides of bowl. Turn out onto a floured surface. Knead 8 to 10 minutes until smooth and elastic. Place in a greased bowl, turning once to grease top. Cover with a tea towel. Let stand in oven with light on and door closed for about 1 hour until doubled in size. Punch dough down. Divide into 2 equal portions. Divide each portion into 3 pieces. Roll each piece into an 18 inch (45 cm) strand. Pinch 3 ends together. Braid strands loosely, then pinch remaining 3 ends together. Place on a greased baking sheet. Cover each pan with a tea towel. Let stand in oven with light on and door closed for about 30 minutes until doubled in size. Bake in 375°F (190°C) oven for 25 to 30 minutes. Turn out onto racks to cool. Brush warm tops with remaining 2 tsp. (10 mL) butter. Makes 2 loaves. Each loaf cuts into 18 slices.

1 slice: *120 Calories; 3.5 g Total Fat (1 g Mono, 0 g Poly, 2 g Sat); 10 mg Cholesterol; 18 g Carbohydrate (trace Fibre, 2 g Sugar); 4 g Protein; 140 mg Sodium*

Hamburger Buns

No one really knows which culture should get credit for creating the hamburger patty (some soures say the Mongols under Kublai Khan, others say Germans from Hamburg), or who first thought to serve it in a bun (though the Americans like to take credit for that bit of innovation), but once the idea was born, there was no stopping it. Grilled, pan-fried or baked, chicken, beef or vegetarian, we love them all. Canadians rate burgers as their favourite food to barbecue, but a burger is only as good as the bun in which it is served. Mass-produced buns do not do our beloved burgers justice, so for your next backyard barbecue, whip up a batch of these tasty buns. The dough can also be used to make hot dog buns.

Sugar	**1/2 cup**	**125 mL**
Warm water	**3 cups**	**750 mL**
1/4 oz. (7 g) packages active dry yeast	**2**	**2**
Large eggs	**2**	**2**
Cooking oil	**1/2 cup**	**125 mL**
Salt	**1 tsp.**	**5 mL**
All-purpose flour	**9 cups**	**2.25 L**
Sesame seeds	**2 tbsp.**	**30 mL**

Stir sugar in warm water in a large bowl. Sprinkle yeast over top. Let stand 10 minutes. Stir to dissolve yeast.

Mix in eggs, cooking oil and salt. Work in enough flour so that dough pulls away from sides of bowl. Turn out onto a floured surface. Knead 8 to 10 minutes until smooth and elastic. Cut off 4 oz. (133 g) pieces of dough, about the size of a tennis ball. Sprinkle with sesame seeds. Flatten slightly with your hand. Place on baking sheets 2 inches (5 cm) apart. Cover with a tea towel. Let stand in oven with light on and door closed for about 1 1/4 hours until doubled in size. Bake in 375°F (190°C) oven for about 20 minutes. Turn out onto a rack to cool. Makes 24 buns.

1 serving: *230 Calories; 5 g Total Fat (3 g Mono, 1.5 g Poly, 0.5 g Sat); 20 mg Cholesterol; 40 g Carbohydrate (1 g Fibre, 4 g Sugar); 6 g Protein; 105 mg Sodium*

Air Buns

Air buns are sweet dinner rolls that get their name from their light, fluffy texture. They are the perfect accompaniment to soups, stews or any meal served with gravy, where they can be used to sop up any liquid left on the dish. In the early days of Canadian settlement, it was a challenge for newly arrived immigrants to eke a living off the land. When possible, people of a particular heritage tended to settle in areas where their culture already had a presence. In that way they could still feel a connection to ther homeland even as they worked to build a life in their new one. These rural communities were tight-knit, with neighbours working together to tackle labour-intensive tasks like harvesting the crops or branding cattle. This fail-safe recipe would have been a staple in homestead kitchens across the land. It yields a lot of buns, perfect for a farm (or ranch) wife with a throng of hungry hands to feed. These buns keep well and can also be frozen for later use.

Hot water	**4 cups**	**1 L**
Butter (or hard margarine), cut up	**1/2 cup**	**125 mL**
Sugar	**1/2 cup**	**125 mL**
White vinegar	**1 tbsp.**	**15 mL**
Salt	**1 tsp.**	**5 mL**
All-purpose flour	**4 cups**	**1 L**
1/4 oz. (7 g) package instant yeast	**1**	**1**
All-purpose flour	**7 1/2 cups**	**1.9 L**
Butter (or hard margarine), softened	**2 tbsp.**	**30 mL**

Measure first 5 ingredients into a large bowl. Stir to melt butter. Cool to lukewarm.

Combine first amount of flour and yeast in a small bowl. Beat slowly into wet ingredients. Beat until smooth. Work in enough remaining flour so that dough pulls away from sides of bowl. Place in a greased bowl, turning once to grease top. Cover with a tea towel. Let stand in oven with light on and door closed for 1 to 1 1/2 hours until doubled in size. Punch dough down. Cover with a tea towel. Let stand in oven with light on and door closed for 1 hour. Punch dough down. Shape into 60 egg-size balls. Place on greased baking sheets 2 inches (5 cm) apart. Cover with a tea towel. Let stand in oven with light on and door closed for 3 hours. Bake in 350°F (175°C) oven for about 20 minutes until golden brown. Turn out onto racks to cool.

Brush warm tops with butter. Makes 60 buns.

1 bun: *50 Calories; 1.5 g Total Fat (0 g Mono, 0 g Poly, 1 g Sat); trace Cholesterol; 8 g Carbohydrate (0 g Fibre, 2 g Sugar); trace Protein; 40 mg Sodium*

Buttermilk Rolls

Back in the early days of European settlement in Canada, every farm would have had access to buttermilk, the slightly sour milk leftover from the process of churning butter. A frugal farm cook would have put the buttermilk to good use in the kitchen, using it in biscuits and an assortment of breads. The buttermilk of today differs from that which our ancestors would have used (modern buttermilk being made of pasteurized milk with live cultures added) but it is still excellent in many baked goods, giving these rolls a buttery tang and a light, fluffy texture. These rolls are ideal as dinner rolls smeared with butter and are often served at Thanksgiving. They are also great to use as the base for ham and cheese sandwiches.

Buttermilk, at room temperature	**1 1/2 cups**	**375 mL**
Sugar	**2 tbsp.**	**30 mL**
Active dry yeast	**2 1/4 tsp.**	**11 mL**
Bread flour	**3 cups**	**750 mL**
Kosher salt	**1 tsp.**	**5 mL**
Instant mashed potato flakes	**1/2 cup**	**125 mL**
Unsalted butter	**2 tbsp.**	**30 mL**
Cornmeal	**2 tbsp.**	**30 mL**

In a large bowl, combine first 7 ingredients and knead for 8 to 10 minutes until smooth. Cover bowl with plastic wrap and let stand in oven with light on and door closed for about 1 hour, until doubled in size.

Turn dough out onto a well-floured surface. Divide into 12 equal pieces and roll each piece into a ball. Place balls on a baking sheet sprinkled with cornmeal and cover with plastic wrap. Let stand in refrigerator overnight or up to 24 hours. Bake buns in 350°F (175°C) oven until browned, about 25 minutes. Transfer to a wire rack to cool. Makes 12 rolls.

***1 roll:** 200 Calories; 3 g Total Fat (0.5 g Mono, 0 g Poly, 1.5 g Sat); 10 mg Cholesterol; 36 g Carbohydrate (1 g Fibre, 2 g Sugar); 5 g Protein; 220 mg Sodium*

Refrigerator Rolls

Refrigerator rolls, also known as icebox rolls, are convenient and exceptionally easy to make. They get their name from the dough's ability to be left in the fridge for up to 5 days before being baked. Modern-day refrigerator rolls are based on old French bread recipes, which were often made into rolls. The main difference between the rolls and the bread is the addition of eggs, milk and butter.

Sugar	**1/4 cup**	**60 mL**
Vegetable shortening	**3 tbsp.**	**45 mL**
Salt	**1 1/2 tsp.**	**7.5 mL**
Milk	**1 cup**	**250 mL**
1/4 oz. (7 g) package of active dry yeast	**1**	**1**
Lukewarm water	**3/4 cup**	**175 mL**
Large egg, beaten	**1**	**1**
All-purpose flour	**4 cups**	**1 L**

In a large mixing bowl, stir sugar, vegetable shortening and salt together until blended.

In a small saucepan, scald milk. Pour over sugar mixture and set aside to cool to lukewarm.

In a small bowl, stir yeast in water until dissolved. Add egg and mix until well blended. Stir into milk mixture.

Add 2 cups (500 mL) flour. Gradually stir in as much of remaining flour as needed to make dough into an elastic ball. Place dough into a well-greased bowl, turning once to grease top. Cover bowl with plastic wrap and refrigerate for at least 8 hours or up to 5 days. When ready to bake, divide dough into 20 pieces. Shape each piece into a tight ball, keeping rest of dough pieces covered with plastic wrap to prevent drying. Place shaped balls 1/2 inch (12 mm) apart on well-greased baking pans. Cover and let stand in oven with light on and door closed for 1 hour until doubled in size. Bake in 375°F (190°C) oven for 15 to 20 minutes until golden brown. Makes 20 rolls.

1 roll: *130 Calories; 2.5 g Total Fat (0 g Mono, 0 g Poly, 0.5 g Sat); 10 mg Cholesterol; 24 g Carbohydrate (trace Fibre, 3 g Sugar); 4 g Protein; 190 mg Sodium*

Kaiser Rolls

This famous roll comes to us from the Viennese society of the mid-19th century. The roll was called the Kaiser-Semmel (imperial roll) in honour of the much-loved Kaiser Franz Joseph I of the Austro-Hungarian Empire. The distinct star-shaped top is said to represent a crown. The kaiser roll is recognized as the first bread to be made without a starter; instead, beer yeast was added to the dough, giving the rolls a sweeter flavour than could be achieved from a starter. It was showcased at the International Exposition of 1867 in Paris, where it was hugely popular.

All-purpose flour	**6 cups**	**1.5 L**
Instant yeast	**3 tsp.**	**15 mL**
Sugar	**3 tsp.**	**15 mL**
Salt	**2 1/2 tsp.**	**12 mL**
Large eggs	**2**	**2**
Unsalted butter	**4 tbsp.**	**60 mL**
Water	**1 1/2 cups**	**375 mL**

Add all ingredients to a large mixing bowl and stir until dough comes together. Knead dough for 5 minutes. Allow it to rest for 10 minutes. Knead for another 5 minutes. Place into a greased bowl, turning once to grease the top, and cover with plastic wrap. Let dough stand in oven with light on and door closed until doubled in size, about 1 hour. Transfer dough to a lightly floured work surface and divide it into 12 equal pieces. Shape pieces into round balls and place them on a lightly greased baking sheet. Working with one ball of dough at a time, cut a cross shape with a knife into each roll. Place rolls cut side down on a baking sheet. Cover with a tea towel and let stand in oven with light on and door closed for 1 hour. Turn rolls cut side up. Bake in 425°F (220°C) oven for 15 to 17 minutes, until golden brown. Transfer to a wire rack to cool. Makes 12 rolls.

***1 roll:** 280 Calories; 5 g Total Fat (1.5 g Mono, 0.5 g Poly, 3 g Sat); 45 mg Cholesterol; 49 g Carbohydrate (2 g Fibre, 1 g Sugar); 8 g Protein; 500 mg Sodium*

Mantou

The Chinese cook their breads not by baking but by steaming them (traditionally in wicker baskets but now often in a steamer). These unique rolls come from Northern China, where wheat rather than rice predominates. In the north, they are traditionally served as part of a meal; in the south, bread is not a staple of the diet, but these rolls are often served in restaurants or as street food. They are also eaten dipped in sweetened condensed milk.

Sugar	**1 tbsp.**	**15 mL**
Warm water	**1 1/4 cups**	**300 mL**
1/4 oz. (7 g) package of active dry yeast	**1**	**1**
All-purpose flour	**3 1/4 cups**	**800 mL**

Stir sugar and water together in a medium bowl. Sprinkle in yeast and let stand for 10 minutes. Stir to dissolve yeast

Slowly add flour, stirring and then beating vigorously until dough forms and pulls away from sides of bowl. Turn dough out onto a lightly floured surface and knead for about 4 minutes. Place dough in a greased bowl, turning to coat top. Cover with waxed paper and a tea towel and let stand in oven with light on and door closed for about 1 1/2 hours. Punch dough down, remove from bowl and cut into 12 equal pieces with a sharp knife. Shape pieces into balls about 2 inches (5 cm) in diameter. Place balls about 2 inches (5 cm) apart on a piece of cheesecloth that fits into your steamer. Let rise for 10 minutes. Place tray in steamer and steam over boiling water for 20 minutes. Remove and serve warm. Makes 12 buns.

1 bun: *120 Calories; 0 g Total Fat (0 g Mono, 0 g Poly, 0 g Sat); 0 mg Cholesterol; 26 g Carbohydrate (1 g Fibre, 0 g Sugar); 4 g Protein; 0 mg Sodium*

Mantou can also be deep-fried and are then referred to as golden mantou for their rich colour.

Croissants

Although the croissant might bring to mind relaxing at an outdoor café, sipping a café au lait, the Eiffel Tower providing a lovely backdrop as you watch the Parisian crowds pass by, this tasty pastry actually originated in Austria. A number of legends describe why the croissant was created; however, whether you believe that it was in celebration of victory over the Turks, an attempt to curb Marie Antoinette's homesickness or a Viennese baker trying to set up shop in Paris, the croissant's Austrian roots are undeniable. So why, then, do we think of croissants as the quintessential French pastry? Well, Austria might have provided the design, but France provided the flair. At the hands of French bakers, the croissant transformed from a bread-like crescent into the light, flaky pastry that we know and love today. Best when freshly baked, croissants are typically eaten for breakfast in France, but in Canada we make room for them any time of day.

Sugar	**1 tsp.**	**5 mL**
Warm water	**1/4 cup**	**60 mL**
1/4 oz. (7 g) package of active dry yeast	**1**	**1**
Milk	**1 1/2 cups**	**375 mL**
Sugar	**1/3 cup**	**75 mL**
Salt	**1 1/2 tsp.**	**7 mL**
Large egg	**1**	**1**
All-purpose flour	**1 cups**	**250 mL**
Butter (or hard margarine), melted	**1/4 cup**	**60 mL**
Cold butter (not margarine)	**1 cup**	**250 mL**
All-purpose flour	**4 cups**	**1 L**
Large egg	**1**	**1**
Water	**1 tbsp.**	**15 mL**

Stir first amount of sugar and warm water together in a small bowl. Sprinkle yeast over top. Let stand 10 minutes. Stir to dissolve yeast.

Combine milk, remaining sugar, salt, 1 egg, the first amount of flour and melted butter in a medium bowl. Add yeast mixture. Beat until smooth.

In a large bowl, cut cold butter into remaining flour until it is the size of large shelled peanuts. Add yeast mixture. Use a rubber spatula to fold together just until flour is moistened. Divide dough into 4 equal portions. Place all 4 portions in bowl. Cover with a tea towel. Chill in refrigerator for 15 minutes. Remove 1 portion at a time from refrigerator. Roll on lightly floured board into 16 inch (40 cm) circle. Cut into 8 wedges. Starting at

(continued on next page)

wide end, roll loosely towards point. Arrange, point side down, on ungreased baking sheet, shaping into a crescent. Leave a 2 inch (5 cm) space between each roll. Cover with a tea towel. Let stand in oven with light on and door closed for 1 1/2 to 2 hours until almost doubled in size.

Using a fork, beat remaining egg with water in a small bowl. Brush over each roll. Bake in 375°F (190°C) oven for about 15 minutes. Remove to racks to cool. Makes 32 croissants.

1 croissant: *150 Calories; 8 g Total Fat (2 g Mono, 0 g Poly, 4.5 g Sat); 35 mg Cholesterol; 18 g Carbohydrate (trace Fibre, 3 g Sugar); 3 g Protein; 125 mg Sodium*

Montréal-style Bagels

The history of the bagel in Canada is a bit murky, but it is commonly accepted that Jewish settlers from Poland (or eastern Europe) brought the Bar Mitzvah faves to North America around 1880. Two men are named as the potential father of the Montréal bagel—Isadore Shlafman and Chaim Seligman. Shalfman opened Montréal's first bagel bakery in 1919, but both men were selling their wares from carts on the street long before the bagelerie's doors first opened. Seligman opened his bagelerie in 1957, and the two establishments have been vying for supremacy ever since.

1/4 oz. (7 g) package of active dry yeast	**1**	**1**
Warm water	**1 1/2 cups**	**375 mL**
Sugar	**1 tsp.**	**5 mL**
Salt	**2 tsp.**	**10 mL**
Vegetable oil	**3 tsp.**	**15 mL**
Honey	**1/4 cup**	**60 mL**
Large egg	**1**	**1**
Egg yolk	**1**	**1**
All-purpose flour	**4 1/2 cups**	**1 L**
Poppy seeds	**1 cup**	**250 mL**
Baking soda	**1 tbsp.**	**15 mL**
Honey	**1/3 cup**	**75 mL**

Stir yeast into warm water in a large bowl. Cover bowl with a tea towel and let stand for 5 to 7 minutes, until bubbly. Stir in sugar, salt, oil, first amount of honey, egg and yolk. Add 1 cup (250 mL) flour and stir until combined. Add remaining flour and stir until a dough forms.

Place dough on a floured surface and knead for about 10 minutes, adding flour as necessary, until dough is smooth. Cover with a bowl and let stand for 35 minutes.

Pour poppy seeds into a shallow dish. Set aside. Heat water in a large pot until boiling. Add baking soda and remaining honey and reduce heat to a simmer. Cook bagels, 2 at a time, for 1 minute per side. Remove with a slotted spoon and dip one side into poppy seeds. Place on a baking sheet. Bake in 500°F (260°C) oven until they begin to brown on bottom, about 10 to 12 minutes. Turn bagels over and bake for another 5 to 8 minutes, until golden brown. Makes 12 bagels.

***1 bagel:** 370 Calories; 12 g Total Fat (3 g Mono, 3 g Poly, 1 g Sat); 35 mg Cholesterol; 56 g Carbohydrate (6 g Fibre, 13 g Sugar); 11 g Protein; 1250 mg Sodium*

Another infamous rivalry is that of the Montréal bagel versus its New York counterpart. Traditional Montréal bagels are made with malt, honey and egg but no salt. They are hand-rolled and boiled in honey water before being baked in wood-fired ovens. They differ from New York bagels in that they are smaller, sweeter and have crispier crust (and Montréal bagel aficionados would say, are much better).

Pretzels

Although a number of countries claim to be their birthplace, pretzels most likely originated in Germany, where the earliest record of the bread dates back to the early 12th century. Possible explanations abound for the characteristic pretzel shape. Some suggest that it represents arms crossed in prayer (historically, praying monks crossed their arms and placed their hands on their shoulders). Others believe that the three holes represent the holy trinity, and a third theory suggests that the holes had a practical purpose, allowing the pretzels to be hung on strings or sticks to be sold. The Pennsylvania Dutch are credited with bringing the pretzel to the New World, where its popularity spread throughout the U.S. and into Canada.

Sugar	**1 tsp.**	**5 mL**
Warm water	**1/4 cup**	**60 mL**
1/4 oz. (7 g) package of active dry yeast	**1**	**1**
Warm water	**1 1/2 cups**	**375 mL**
All-purpose flour	**4 1/2 cups**	**1.1 L**
Salt	**1/2 tsp.**	**2 mL**
Large egg white	**1**	**1**
Water	**1 tbsp.**	**15 mL**
Coarse salt	**1 tbsp.**	**15 mL**

Stir sugar into first amount of warm water in a small bowl. Sprinkle yeast over top. Let stand for 10 minutes. Stir to dissolve yeast.

Combine remaining warm water, flour and salt in a large bowl. Add yeast mixture. Add a bit more flour if needed so dough isn't too sticky. Turn out onto floured surface. Knead 8 to 10 minutes until smooth and elastic. Place in a greased bowl, turning once to grease top. Cover with a tea towel. Let stand in oven with light on and door closed about 45 minutes until doubled in size. Punch dough down. Roll into a log. Cut into 9 portions. Roll each portion into 1/2 inch (12 mm) thick strand. Shape each strand into a pretzel on greased baking sheets.

In a small bowl, beat egg white and water with a fork. Brush over pretzels. Sprinkle pretzels with salt. Bake in 450°F (230°C) oven for about 15 minutes. Turn out onto racks to cool. Makes 9 pretzels.

1 pretzel: *240 Calories; 1 g Total Fat (0 g Mono, 0.5 g Poly, 0 g Sat); 0 mg Cholesterol; 49 g Carbohydrate (2 g Fibre, trace Sugar); 7 g Protein; 480 mg Sodium*

Grissini

Torino, in northwestern Italy, is known as the birthplace of grissini, the original breadstick. Theories abound regarding the origin of this bread, but the most popular seems to be that a baker in the late 17th century was tasked with creating a bread for a sick young duke, who was unable to tolerate food. The baker took the dough for a traditional local bread and stretched it long and thin so that when baked it would be crisp, and therefore easy to digest. The duke recovered, and the breadsticks credited with curing him grew in popularity, eventually spreading throughout Italy and beyond. Today they are often eaten as an accompaniment to a glass of wine or as an appetizer, sometimes wrapped with a slice of prosciutto. In Canada, grissini can be found in most Italian centres and even some mainstream supermarkets. But, of course, nothing beats homemade.

White bread flour	**2 cups**	**500 mL**
Salt	**1 1/2 tsp.**	**7 mL**
Sugar	**1 tsp.**	**5 mL**
Lukewarm water	**2/3 cup**	**150 mL**
1/4 oz. (7 g) package of active dry yeast	**1**	**1**
Extra virgin olive oil,	**2 tbsp.**	**30 mL**
Sesame seeds	**2 tbsp.**	**30 mL**

Combine flour and salt in a large bowl and make a well in centre.

Combine sugar and water in a small bowl. Sprinkle yeast over top. Let stand 10 minutes. Stir to dissolve yeast. Add to well.

Add oil and stir until a soft dough forms. Turn out onto a lightly floured surface and knead until smooth, about 10 minutes. Roll out to a 6 x 8 inch (15 x 20 cm) rectangle. Brush with 1 tbsp. (15 mL) oil and cover with lightly greased plastic wrap. Let stand in oven with light on and door closed until doubled in size, about 1 hour.

Pour sesame seeds onto a plate or shallow bowl. Cut dough into 30 strips. Gently stretch each strip to 9 inches (23 cm) long. Roll in sesame seeds and place about 1/2 inch (12 mm) apart on a lightly greased baking sheet. Brush with remaining 2 tbsp. (30 mL) oil and let stand, covered, in oven with light on and door closed for about 10 minutes. Bake in 400°F (200°C) oven for 15 to 20 minutes, until pale golden and crisp. Transfer to a wire rack to cool. Makes 30 grissini.

1 breadstick: *50 Calories; 2.5 g Total Fat (1 g Mono, 0 g Poly, 0 g Sat); 0 mg Cholesterol; 7 g Carbohydrate (0 g Fibre, 0 g Sugar); 1 g Protein; 115 mg Sodium*

Pizza Dough

Pizza is an Italian specialty that most North Americans have happily adopted. The word pizza literally means "pie" in Italian. In Italy, pizzerias everywhere bake their own regional specialties in wood-fired brick ovens. This gives the pizzas a unique texture and flavour that is hard to copy here at home. This recipe for pizza crust makes a thin, bread-like crust that you can top with your favourite ingredients. You can also bake the crust untopped for 8 to 10 minutes, then reheat it with toppings later.

Lukewarm water	**3/4 cup**	**175 mL**
Sugar	**1 tsp.**	**5 mL**
1/4 oz. (7 g) package of active dry yeast	**1**	**1**
All-purpose flour	**3 cups**	**750 mL**
Salt	**1/4 tsp.**	**1 mL**
Vegetable oil	**2 tbsp.**	**30 mL**

Pour water into a medium bowl and add sugar, stirring until dissolved. Sprinkle yeast over top and let stand until foamy, about 10 minutes.

Meanwhile combine flour and salt in a large bowl. Set aside.

Add oil to yeast mixture and stir with a fork until blended. Slowly add to flour, mixing until dough starts to form a ball (you may not use all the yeast mixture). Place dough on a lightly floured board and knead 5 to 8 minutes until dough is smooth and shiny. Place in a greased bowl, turning to coat top. Cover and let stand 15 minutes. Place dough on lightly floured surface and roll with a heavy rolling pin into a circle about 1/4 inch (6 mm) thick. Place on a lightly greased pizza pan. Top with your favourite tomato sauce and ingredients. Bake in 400°F (200°C) oven for 15 to 20 minutes. Makes 1 large crust. Cuts into 14 slices.

***1 slice:** 280 Calories; 6 g Total Fat (1.5 g Mono, 1.5 g Poly, 2.5 g Sat); 35 mg Cholesterol; 49 g Carbohydrate (2 g Fibre, 12 g Sugar); 7 g Protein; 160 mg Sodium*

Despite its name, the Hawaiian pizza is actually a Canadian invention, but who is responsible for its creation is a matter of debate. Some believe that Sam Panopoulos, in 1962, was experimenting with different pizza options for his fledgling restaurant the Satellite, in Chatham, Ontario, when he came up with the winning combination of back bacon (or ham) and pineapple. Others believe the Hawaiian was invented at Boston Pizza in Edmonton around 1973.

Focaccia

Focaccia gets its name from the Latin focacius, *meaning "hearth." It is believed to date back to at least the time of the Etruscans, when it was cooked on heated earthenware or on the hearth of a fire. Focaccia is often thought of as the precursor to pizza, and it is just as flexible. This bread is baked throughout Italy, with every region having its own favourite toppings. Simple focaccia might have nothing more than a sprinkling of coarse salt, but fresh herbs, veggies, cured meats or different types of cheese are often added as well. Don't be tempted to overload this bread with toppings, though, or you'll weigh down the dough.*

Sugar	**1 tsp.**	**5 mL**
Warm water	**1/4 cup**	**60 mL**
1/4 oz. (7 g) package of active dry yeast	**1**	**1**
All-purpose flour	**3 1/4 cups**	**800 mL**
Salt	**1 tsp.**	**5 mL**
Olive oil (or cooking oil)	**2 tsp.**	**10 mL**
Water	**1 cup**	**250 mL**
Sliced black olives	**1/2 cup**	**125 mL**
Sun-dried tomatoes	**1/4 cup**	**60 mL**
Crumbled feta cheese	**1/2 cup**	**125 mL**
Grated mozzarella cheese	**1/2 cup**	**125 mL**
Grated Parmesan cheese	**2 tbsp.**	**30 mL**

Combine sugar and first amount of warm water in a small bowl. Sprinkle yeast over top. Let stand 10 minutes. Stir to dissolve yeast.

Combine flour and salt in a large bowl. Make a well in centre. Add yeast mixture to well. Stir with a spoon until mixed. Make a well in centre.

Add olive oil and remaining water to well and stir. Turn out onto a floured surface. Knead for 8 to 10 minutes until smooth and elastic. Place in a greased bowl, turning once to coat top. Cover with a tea towel. Let stand in oven with light on and door closed for 1 to 1 1/2 hours until doubled in size. Punch dough down. Place on a greased baking sheet and press or roll out to an oval.

Combine olives, tomatoes and all cheeses in a medium bowl. Sprinkle over dough. Bake in 400°F (200°C) oven for about 25 minutes. Serve warm or cold. Makes 1 loaf. Cuts into 18 wedges.

1 wedge: *120 Calories; 3 g Total Fat (1 g Mono, 0 g Poly, 1 g Sat); 5 mg Cholesterol; 19 g Carbohydrate (trace Fibre, trace Sugar); 4 g Protein; 250 mg Sodium*

Naan

Although the word naan *is of Persian origin, translating simply to "bread," we associate the name with the soft, puffy flatbreads we see in Indian restaurants. Naan is one of the few leavened Indian breads; the leavening agent can be yeast, baking soda or baking powder, but the ingredient that really sets these breads apart is the yogurt, which ferments and gives the bread a light, bubbly appearance. Traditionally these flatbreads would be cooked in large clay ovens, called* tandoors, *where the dough would be stuck to the inside wall of the oven and peeled off when cooked, making the bread crispy in some places and soft and chewy in others. You can't get quite the same texture from your home oven, but this recipe is the next best thing. Try cooking the naan on your barbecue for a more authentic flavour.*

Large eggs	**2**	**2**
Plain yogurt	**1/4 cup**	**60 mL**
Milk	**3/4 cup**	**175 mL**
Cooking oil	**1/4 cup**	**60 mL**
All-purpose flour	**4 cups**	**1 L**
Sugar	**1 tbsp.**	**15 mL**
Baking powder	**1 tbsp.**	**15 mL**
Baking soda	**1/2 tsp.**	**2 mL**
Salt	**1 1/2 tsp.**	**7 mL**

Beat eggs in a large bowl until frothy. Stir in yogurt, milk and cooking oil.

Combine remaining 5 ingredients in a separate bowl. Stir into egg mixture. Turn out onto a floured surface. Knead 8 to 10 times until dough is smooth. Cut into 30 pieces about the size of a golf ball. Cover with a damp tea towel. Let stand for 1 hour. On a lightly floured surface, roll or pat each ball into a 6 inch (15 cm) circle. Arrange on greased baking sheets. Bake in 450°F (230°C) oven for about 3 to 4 minutes until puffed and browned. Makes 30 naan.

1 naan: *90 Calories; 2.5 g Total Fat (1.5 g Mono, 0.5 g Poly, 0 g Sat); 15 mg Cholesterol; 14 g Carbohydrate (0 g Fibre, trace Sugar); 3 g Protein; 180 mg Sodium*

Pita

This flatbread has been baked in the Middle East for many centuries. It has few ingredients, a simple method and can be baked in an oven or on hot rocks by a campfire. The pockets that develop are great to stuff with vegetables or meats, or simply spread with butter. The breads will be hard when removed from the oven but the crust will soften and flatten as they cool. If you can't use them up within a day, freeze the rest because they quickly lose their freshness.

1/4 oz (7 g) package of active dry yeast	**1**	**1**
Warm water	**1 1/4 cups**	**300 mL**
Salt	**2 tsp.**	**10 mL**
All-purpose flour	**2 cups**	**500 mL**
All-purpose flour	**2 cups**	**500 mL**

In a mixing bowl, dissolve yeast in warm water. Let stand for 5 minutes. Stir in salt and 2 cups of flour. Beat vigorously with the electric mixer for 3 minutes.

Add remaining flour, 1/2 cup (125 mL) at a time, mixing first with a spoon then with your hands. A rough, shaggy mass should develop. Turn dough out onto a lightly floured surface. Knead until dough is soft, about 8 minutes. Divide dough into 6 pieces and form each into a round ball. Using a rolling pin, flatten each ball into a circle about 4 inches (10 cm) in diameter and 1/4 inch (6 mm) thick. Alternatively, place ball between two pieces of waxed paper, then flatten with a pie plate. Place rounds together on work surface and cover with a towel or waxed paper. Let stand for 45 minutes or until they are slightly puffy. Turn rounds upside down onto a lightly greased baking sheet. Bake in 500°F (260°C) oven for 15 to 18 minutes until light brown and puffed in centre. Remove from pan and place on wire racks to cool. Makes 6 pitas.

1 pita: *310 Calories; 1 g Total Fat (0 g Mono, 0 g Poly, 0 g Sat); 0 mg Cholesterol; 64 g Carbohydrate (2 g Fibre, 0 g Sugar); 9 g Protein; 780 mg Sodium*

Chapati

Most people think of naan as the staple bread in India, but chapatis are actually more common because you need a tandoor to make naan, which few people have, but chapatis can be cooked over an open fire. Indian immigrants to Canada could not have recreated authentic naan in their new land, but chapatis would have been no problem. These whole wheat flatbreads are served hot alongside a main meal; bite-sized pieces are torn off and folded around the food to scoop it up as you would with a spoon.

Whole wheat flour	**1 1/2 cups**	**375 mL**
All-purpose flour	**3/4 cup**	**175 mL**
Salt	**1/4 tsp.**	**1 mL**
Ghee or vegetable oil	**1 tbsp.**	**15 mL**
Water	**1 cup**	**250 mL**

In a large bowl, combine whole wheat flour, all-purpose flour and salt. Add ghee and mix well. Make a well in centre.

Add enough water to make a soft dough. Gather all dough into a ball in bowl. Stretch and knead dough until it is smooth and sides of bowl are clean. The more kneading you do, the lighter the bread will be. Cover with plastic wrap and let stand in oven with light on and door closed for 30 to 40 minutes. Turn dough out onto a lightly floured surface. Divide into 10 equal pieces and form each into a ball. Roll out each ball into a 6 inch (15 cm) circle about 1/8 inch (3 mm) thick. Keep uncooked chapatis covered so they don't dry out. Warm 2 ungreased baking sheets in 450°F (230°C) oven. Arrange breads on warmed sheets and bake for 2 minutes until chapatis are firm to the touch. Increase heat to broil and cook for 2 more minutes, until chapatis are puffed up and hollow. Serve immediately. Makes 10 chapatis.

1 chapati: *110 Calories; 2 g Total Fat (0 g Mono, 0 g Poly, 1 g Sat); trace Cholesterol; 20 g Carbohydrate (2 g Fibre, 0 g Sugar); 3 g Protein; 60 mg Sodium*

In the early days of Canadian settlement, the government instituted a discriminatory immigration policy that required immigrants from India to travel directly from a port in India to one in Canada. At the time, no ships made that direct journey, so would-be Indian immigrants were effectively shut out of Canada. This policy was repealed in the 1960s, and since then the Indo-Canadian community has grown into one of the largest and most well-integrated immigrant communities in Canada.

Tortillas

The tortilla is a traditional Mexican bread, resembling a thin, round, unleavened pancake. It has been served in Mexico for many centuries. Even before the Spaniards arrived and introduced wheat and wheat flour, tortillas were made from masa *or ground corn. Nowadays those who make their own tortillas can use* masa harina *(corn flour), wheat flour or, as in this recipe, a mixture of all-purpose flour and cornmeal.*

All-purpose flour	**1 1/2 cups**	**500 mL**
Cornmeal	**1 cup**	**250 mL**
Salt	**1/2 tsp.**	**2 mL**
Water	**1 1/4 cups**	**300 mL**

Combine flour, cornmeal and salt. Stir in just enough water so mixture forms a ball of dough. Place dough onto a lightly floured surface. Knead and pound until smooth and elastic. Cover with a damp tea towel and let rest for 10 minutes. Divide into 1 inch (2.5 cm) balls and on a lightly floured surface roll each into thin 6 inch (15 cm) circles. Bake tortillas on a heated skillet or cast iron frying pan for 2 to 3 minutes per side. Makes 12 tortillas.

***1 tortilla:** 110 Calories; 0 g Total Fat (0 g Mono, 0 g Poly, 0 g Sat); 0 mg Cholesterol; 23 g Carbohydrate (trace Fibre, 0 g Sugar); 3 g Protein; 100 mg Sodium*

Canada hasn't seen as much immigration from Mexico as our neighbours to the south have, but we have developed an appreciation for Mexican cuisine, or rather Tex-Mex cuisine, arising from the cowboy era when *vaqueros* (Mexican cowboys) worked alongside Canadian and American cowboys driving cattle across the prairies.

Lavash

Lavash is an Armenian flatbread that is widespread throughout the Middle East. In Armenia, it has enormous cultural significance. In keeping with tradition, it is baked by sticking the dough against the inside wall of a cylindrical clay oven, called a tonir, *which is built into the floor of a bake house. Because it is labour intensive, lavash is baked only periodically throughout the year, and the occasion is a community event. Men are responsible for lighting the fire that heats the* tonir, *and a group of select women bake the bread. Lavash is soft when it comes out of the* tonir *but crisps up as it cools. Dry lavash can keep for months and is restored by sprinkling it with water. Although lavash is now produced commercially throughout much of the world, in Armenia traditional* tonir-*baked lavash is still much preferred. To bake a slightly more authentic lavash, try cooking it on a baking stone instead of a sheet.*

All-purpose flour	**2 1/2 cups**	**625 mL**
Sugar	**1 tsp.**	**5 mL**
Salt	**1 tsp.**	**5 mL**
Water	**2/3 cup**	**150 mL**
Egg white (large)	**1**	**1**
Butter (or hard margarine), melted	**2 tbsp.**	**30 mL**
Egg white (large)	**1**	**1**
Sesame seeds	**2 tbsp.**	**30 mL**

Combine flour, sugar and salt in a large bowl.

Add water, first egg white and butter. Mix until a stiff dough forms. Divide dough into 10 balls. Roll each out on a lightly floured surface until paper thin. Place on an ungreased baking sheet.

Beat remaining egg white and brush over dough. Sprinkle with sesame seeds. Bake in 400°F (200°C) oven for about 10 to 12 minutes until browned. Makes 10 lavash.

***1 lavash:** 150 Calories; 3.5 g Total Fat (1 g Mono, 0.5 g Poly, 1.5 g Sat); 5 mg Cholesterol; 25 g Carbohydrate (1 g Fibre, trace Sugar); 4 g Protein; 250 mg Sodium*

Armenians believe that lavash takes on the mood of those who touch it, so only women with happy, positive dispositions are allowed to be part of the baking process.

Poppadoms

Poppadoms, also spelled poppadum or papadam, are thin, crisp, disc-shaped flatbreads made with black gram flour, from black lentils. They originate from both India and Pakistan as an easy, calorie-rich snack and are often found alongside vegetarian dishes. They are especially suitable for dipping in chutney and can be store in a dry, air-tight container for easy eating. In this recipe we've added curry powder to the dough, but you can add any spice you'd like; garlic powder or cayenne are also good choices.

Water	**1 3/4 cup**	**425 mL**
Black gram flour	**3 tsp.**	**15 mL**
Rice flour	**1/2 cup**	**125 mL**
Baking soda	**1 tsp.**	**5 mL**
Salt	**1 tsp.**	**5 mL**
Curry powder	**1 tbsp.**	**15 mL**
Peanut oil	**3 cups**	**750 mL**

Pour water into a pan and add black gram flour, rice flour and baking soda. On low heat, stir mixture continuously for approximately 10 minutes. Spread mixture onto parchment paper using a spatula to spread into circular shapes. Cover with a second sheet of parchment paper and use a rolling pin to roll dough as thin as possible. Remove top layer of parchment paper and place sheets into oven set at its lowest possible temperature for about 2 hours, until crisp.

In a large deep-sided pan or wok, heat oil to 360°F (180°C) and fry each poppadom until puffed and golden, about 2 to 3 minutes. Use a slotted spoon to submerge poppadom in oil as they fry to make sure they cook evenly on both sides. Transfer poppadoms to a tray lined with paper towel to dry and cool. Makes 10 poppadoms.

***1 poppadom:** 70 Calories; 4 g Total Fat (2 g Mono, 1.5 g Poly, 0.5 g Sat); 0 mg Cholesterol; 7 g Carbohydrate (0 g Fibre, 0 g Sugar); trace Protein; 360 mg Sodium*

Why They Came...the Chinese

The first record of Chinese people setting foot in what is now Canada comes from the 1780s, when a crew of 50 arrived with the British merchant John Meares, who was actively trading with Asia and wanted to set up a trading post at Nootka Sound. When Meares moved on, many of his Chinese crew went with him. Records from the time are a bit sketchy, but it seems that the men who stayed behind married local Indigenous women and settled nicely into their new land.

The first real influx of Chinese immigrants began with the Fraser River Gold Rush in the late 1850s. Many Chinese men had come to North America during the California Gold Rush, and with the discovery of gold in BC (then called New Caledonia) turned their sights northward. Before long, people were arriving directly from China to try their hand at panning for gold. Victoria, at the time, was the main port of entry for ships coming from Asia, and many new arrivals settle there, forming Canada's first Chinatown (which is now the second oldest in North America, beaten only by San Francisco).

The next wave of Chinese immigrants came in the 1880s to help build the final leg of the Canadian Pacific Railway. The Conservatives under John A. Macdonald promised the Canadian public a railway stretching from the east coast to the west, linking far-flung communities with the industrial powers in Ontario. The railway was to be completed within 10 years, but building the western section was labour intensive and there were not enough workers in Canada to get the job done. Outside help was needed, so labourers were brought in, some from the U.S., some from Europe, but most from China. Between 1881 and 1884, about 17,000 Chinese workers arrived in BC. These men were given the most dangerous jobs, blasting away rock and digging tunnels, yet received only about half the wage their fellow white workers were paid. Once the railway was complete, the workers were left with no jobs and began to disperse throughout the country in search of employment. Many founded their own businesses, particularly laundries or restaurants, which did not require much money to start or a proficiency in English. Others were drawn to other natural resource extraction industries, such as coal mining or logging.

Chinese people faced enormous discrimination in this country, with many Canadian residents affronted by what they thought were too many immigrants arriving from China. As a result, the government established a Chinese head tax in 1885; at a time when Europeans were being enticed to Canada with the promise of free land, the Chinese had to pay $50 to enter the country. When that tactic did not stem the flow of immigrants enough to appease the disgruntled public, the government enacted the Chinese Immigration Act, also known as the Chinese Exclusion Act, in 1923. Until it was repealed in 1947, only a handful of Chinese merchants were allowed to move to Canada.

Today, the Chinese community in Canada is more than a million strong, with a presence in every province, particularly in BC and Ontario.

Green Onion Cakes

Green onion cakes, or chung yao beng, are a traditional Chinese bread, often served on Chinese New Year. They are crispy on the outside, flaky in the inside, yet chewy with a distinct green onion flavour. Summer in Edmonton would not be the same without these cakes. First appearing in the city in the 1980s, green onion cakes have become a staple at many Edmonton events, including the Fringe, the Taste of Edmonton and the Edmonton International Street Performers Festival, where they are typically served with sambal oelek (a type of chili paste). According to Paul A. Lucas, Events Edmonton general manager, "Nobody outside of China has embraced green onion cakes like we have so let's be proud of that." There was even a movement to make the cakes the official food of Edmonton, but to date that has not come to pass.

White bread flour	**3 cups**	**750 mL**
Boiling water	**1 1/4 cups**	**300 mL**
Bunch of green onions	**1**	**1**
Sesame oil	**2 tbsp.**	**30 mL**
Salt, to taste		
Pepper, to taste		
Cooking oil	**1 tbsp.**	**15 mL**

Combine flour and water in a large bowl and stir until dough comes together. Knead dough for 3 to 5 minutes. Place back in bowl, cover with plastic wrap and let stand for 1 hour.

Finely chop green onion. Set aside. Divide dough into 16 portions. Working with one portion at a time, roll dough into a thin circle. Brush with sesame oil and sprinkle with salt, pepper and green onions, using about 1 tsp. (5 mL) per circle. Roll circle into a sausage shape, then coil dough around itself (think of a sleeping snake) to form a circle. Pinch loose end under coil to seal. With a rolling pin, flatten circle into a 1/4 inch (6 mm) disk.

Heat oil in a large frying pan over medium. Fry cakes until they are golden brown, about 2 minutes per side. Makes 16 cakes.

***1 cake:** 120 Calories; 4 g Total Fat (1.5 g Mono, 1.5 g Poly, 0 g Sat); 0 mg Cholesterol; 19 g Carbohydrate (trace Fibre, 0 g Sugar); 3 g Protein; 75 mg Sodium*

Toutons

Toutons are a Newfoundland specialty made of fried white bread dough. They date back to the time when most Newfoundlanders still baked fresh bread everyday in their homes, and originated as a way to use up leftover bread dough. The dough was shaped into flattened circles, much like a pancake, and pan-fried in pork fat. Today toutons are more often fried in butter, margarine or oil. Crispy on the outside and tender and slightly chewy on the inside, toutons are usually eaten for breakfast or brunch, drizzled with molasses and sometimes topped with a pat of butter. They are also sometimes served with scrunchins (fried diced fatback pork) or alongside a plate of baked beans.

Sugar	**3 tsp.**	**15 mL**
Lukewarm water	**1/2 cup**	**125 mL**
1/4 oz. (7 g) package of active dry yeast	**1**	**1**
2% Milk	**1 cup**	**250 mL**
Shortening	**2 tbsp.**	**30 mL**
Cold water	**1/2 cup**	**125 mL**
Salt	**1/2 tbsp.**	**7 mL**
Sugar	**1 tsp.**	**5 mL**
All-purpose flour	**5 1/2 cups**	**1.4 L**
Bacon or pancetta, finely cubed	**1/4 lb.**	**113 g**

Stir first amount of sugar in lukewarm water in a small bowl. Sprinkle yeast over top. Let stand 10 minutes. Stir to dissolve yeast.

Heat milk in a medium saucepan over medium-low until scalded. Add shortening, stirring until melted. Add cold water, salt and remaining sugar. Cool to lukewarm before adding yeast mixture. Stir until blended.

Add 2 cups (500 mL) flour and beat with a wooden spoon until smooth. Gradually add remaining flour until dough is moist and no longer sticks to bowl. Turn out onto a lightly floured surface and knead for at least 10 minutes. Shape dough into a ball and place in a greased bowl, turning once to grease top. Cover with a damp cloth and let stand in oven with light on and door closed until doubled in size. Turn out onto a floured work surface and punch down in middle. Pinch off pieces of dough 1/3 cup (75 ml) at a time and flatten to a 1/2 inch (12 mm) circle.

In a large frying pan, cook bacon until golden brown and crispy. With a slotted spoon, transfer to a plate lined with paper towel to drain. Add toutons to pan and fry in bacon fat until golden on both sides. Garnish with bacon and serve. Makes 24 toutons.

1 touton: *140 Calories; 3.5 g Total Fat (1 g Mono, 0 g Poly, 1 g Sat); trace Cholesterol; 23 g Carbohydrate (trace Fibre, 1 g Sugar); 4 g Protein; 190 mg Sodium*

Buckwheat Pancakes

Pancakes are one of the oldest forms of bread. Archeological evidence indicates that prehistoric people dating back to the Stone Age may have already been eating a pancake prototype, and most civilizations across the globe can count some variety of pancake as part of their culinary repertoire. For early explorers in Canada, pancakes were a staple. They were easy to make, required only a few basic ingredients, and leftovers travelled much better than buns or bread, which would get crushed in the explorers' packs on the trail. Because of the high cost of wheat, pancakes in the past would have often been made with different flours, including buckwheat. Native to Asia and a popular crop in Europe, buckwheat came to Canada with the early European explorers. Because it prefers cool climates and has a short growing season, it was a good match for Manitoban soils, where the majority of Canadian buckwheat is still grown today.

All-purpose flour	**1 1/4 cups**	**300 mL**
Buckwheat flour	**3/4 cup**	**175 mL**
Sugar	**1/4 cup**	**60 mL**
Baking soda	**2 tsp.**	**10 mL**
Ground cardamom	**1/4 tsp.**	**1 mL**
Salt	**1/4 tsp.**	**1 mL**
Large eggs, fork-beaten	**3**	**3**
Milk	**1 1/4 cup**	**300 mL**
Canola oil	**2 tbsp.**	**30 mL**
Canola oil	**1 tsp.**	**5 mL**

Combine first 6 ingredients in a large bowl. Make a well in centre.

Combine remaining 3 ingredients in a medium bowl. Add to well and stir until just moistened. Batter will be lumpy. Heat remaining oil in a large

(continued on next page)

frying pan on medium. Pour batter into pan, using 1/3 cup (75 mL) for each pancake. Cook for about 2 minutes until bubbles form on top and edges appear dry. Turn pancake over. Cook for about 2 minutes until golden. Remove to plate. Cover to keep warm. Repeat with remaining batter, heating more oil if necessary to prevent sticking. Makes 12 pancakes.

1 pancake: *145 Calories; 4 g Total Fat (2 g Mono, 1 g Poly, 0.5 g Sat); 55 mg Cholesterol; 22 g Carbohydrate (trace Fibre, 6 g Sugar); 5 g Protein; 290 mg Sodium*

Beer Bread

It is a common sentiment that at one time beer was safer to drink than water; after all, contaminated water has killed millions of people worldwide, but how many people have died from contaminated beer? The pathogens that live in water are killed during the brewing of beer, and they cannot live in the finished product because of the alcohol and beer's high acidity. This might explain why beer was used to make bread in many countries. Beer and bread are natural bedfellows, and it has been suggested that ale was discovered as a direct result of bread making. When choosing a beer for this recipe, keep in mind that using a dark beer will give you a darker, more beer-flavoured bread.

Whole wheat flour	**3 cups**	**750 mL**
Baking powder	**1 tsp.**	**5 mL**
Baking soda	**1/2 tsp.**	**2 mL**
Salt	**1/2 tsp.**	**2 mL**
Fancy molasses	**2 tbsp.**	**30 mL**
Beer, room temperature	**12 oz.**	**341 mL**
Butter (or hard margarine), softened	**1 tsp.**	**5 mL**

Mix flour, baking powder, baking soda and salt together in a large bowl.

Stir in molasses and beer. The dough will be sticky. Turn out onto a floured surface. Knead for 1 minute. Put into a greased 8 inch (20 cm) round cake pan. Cut lines with a sharp knife 1/2 inch (12 mm) deep marking 6 to 12 wedges. Bake in 325°F (160°C) oven for 40 to 50 minutes until bread pulls away from side of pan. Turn out onto rack to cool.

Brush warm top with butter. Makes 1 loaf. Cuts into 12 slices.

1 slice: *120 Calories; 0.5 g Total Fat (0 g Mono, 0 g Poly, 0 g Sat); 0 mg Cholesterol; 25 g Carbohydrate (4 g Fibre, 2 g Sugar); 4 g Protein; 180 mg Sodium*

Zucchini Bread

Zucchini is native to the Americas, but the variety that most people are familiar with comes from Italy and was most likely brought back to the Americas by early European immigrants. The plant became a garden favourite because it is so easy to grow, but because it is so prolific, come harvest time farmers had a squash surplus. One can heap only so much zucchini onto unsuspecting neighbours, so farm wives had to think of clever ways to use it up. Hence the birth of zucchini bread. Based on the sweet vegetable puddings that were popular in Europe in the Middle Ages, zucchini bread was (and still is) an excellent way to eat zucchini without really realizing that it is there.

Large eggs	**2**	**2**
Cooking oil	**1/2 cup**	**125 mL**
Sugar	**1 cup**	**250 mL**
Grated zucchini, unpeeled	**1 cup**	**250 mL**
Vanilla	**1 tsp.**	**5 mL**
All-purpose flour	**2 cups**	**500 mL**
Baking powder	**1 tsp.**	**5 mL**
Baking soda	**1 tsp.**	**5 mL**
Salt	**1/2 tsp.**	**2 mL**
Cinnamon	**1 tsp.**	**5 mL**

Beat eggs until frothy. Beat in cooking oil and sugar. Add zucchini. Stir in vanilla.

Combine remaining 5 ingredients in a separate bowl. Stir well and pour into zucchini mixture. Stir just to moisten. Pour mixture into greased 9 x 5 x 3 inch (23 x 12.5 x 7.5 cm) loaf pan. Bake for 50 to 60 minutes in 350°F (180°C) oven until a toothpick inserted in centre comes out clean. Let stand 10 minutes, then remove from pan and transfer to a wire rack to cool. Makes 1 loaf. Cuts into 16 slices.

1 slice: *180 Calories; 8 g Total Fat (4.5 g Mono, 2 g Poly, 0.5 g Sat); 25 mg Cholesterol; 25 g Carbohydrate (trace Fibre, 13 g Sugar); 2 g Protein; 180 mg Sodium*

Cornbread

Corn was a staple for the Huron Wendat of Ontario. It was pounded or ground into a coarse flour and made into unleavened bread that was cooked in hot ashes. Early settlers to Canada adopted this bread and added eggs, soured milk, baking soda and a sweetener, transforming it into the cornbread we know today.

All-purpose flour	**1 1/2 cups**	**375 mL**
Yellow cornmeal	**1 cup**	**250 mL**
Sugar	**1/2 cup**	**125 mL**
Baking powder	**2 tsp.**	**10 mL**
Baking soda	**1 tsp.**	**5 mL**
Salt	**1/2 tsp.**	**2 mL**
Large egg	**1**	**1**
Buttermilk	**1 cup**	**250 mL**
Butter (or hard margarine), melted	**1/4 cup**	**60 mL**

Combine first 6 ingredients in a large bowl. Make a well in centre.

Combine remaining 3 ingredients in a small bowl. Add to well and stir until just moistened. Spread in a greased 9 inch round (23 cm) pan. Bake in 350°F (175°C) oven for about 30 minutes until wooden pick inserted in centre comes out clean. Let stand in pan for 5 minutes before removing to wire rack to cool. Makes 1 loaf. Cuts into 12 slices.

***1 piece:** 190 Calories; 4.5 g Total Fat (1 g Mono, 0 g Poly, 2.5 g Sat); 30 mg Cholesterol; 32 g Carbohydrate (trace Fibre, 8 g Sugar); 3 g Protein; 300 mg Sodium*

Steamed Brown Bread

This molasses-rich bread gets its name from the unusual method of steaming, not baking, in a hot water bath. Steaming breads was common practice in the early days of Canadian settlement, when many people did not have an oven and had to rely on an open fire for cooking. Also known as "Maritime Brown Bread," this loaf has a texture more like that of a pudding. It is often cooked in an old coffee can. This bread can be served with baked beans for a homey dinner or enjoyed toasted with butter. You can substitute chopped dried apricots or raisins for the dates.

Whole wheat flour	**1 cup**	**250 mL**
Rye flour	**1 cup**	**250 mL**
Yellow cornmeal	**1 cup**	**250 mL**
Baking soda	**1 1/2 tsp.**	**7 mL**
Salt	**1 tsp.**	**5 mL**
Buttermilk, at room temperature	**1 1/2 cup**	**375 mL**
Fancy molasses	**3/4 cup**	**175 mL**
Unsweetened applesauce	**1/2 cup**	**125 mL**
Chopped dates	**3/4 cup**	**175 mL**

In a large mixing bowl, combine both flours, cornmeal, baking soda and salt. Make a well in centre.

In a separate bowl, combine buttermilk, molasses and applesauce. Add to well and stir to combine. Stir in dates. Divide mixture between greased 28 oz. (796 mL) soup cans and cover with greased 8 inch (20 cm) squares of parchment paper, greased side down. Tie with string, leaving a 1 inch (2.5 cm) space for bread to rise. Place cans on a steamer rack or heatproof trivet in a deep pot or Dutch oven. Pour in enough boiling water to reach halfway up sides of cans. Cover and return to boil over medium heat. Reduce heat to a simmer and cook until toothpick inserted in centre comes out clean, about 2 1/2 hours. Remove bread from cans and transfer to a wire rack to cool. Makes 2 loaves. Each loaf cuts into 12 slices.

***1 slice:** 110 Calories; trace Total Fat (0 g Mono, 0 g Poly, 0 g Sat); 0 mg Cholesterol; 26 g Carbohydrate (2 g Fibre, 10 g Sugar); 2 g Protein; 200 mg Sodium*

Johnny Cakes

A Jamaican twist to the English biscuit, Johnny cakes date back to the days of slavery. Originally known as "journey cakes," because of their portability, these cakes were tucked into Jamaican slaves' lunch to get them through a long day in the fields. They differ from American Johnny cakes, which were made of cornmeal.

All-purpose flour	**2 cups**	**500 mL**
Baking powder	**2 tsp.**	**10 mL**
Salt	**1/4 tsp.**	**1 mL**
Butter (or hard margarine)	**2 tbsp.**	**30 mL**
Water	**1 cup**	**250 mL**
Oil for frying	**3 tbsp.**	**45 mL**

Combine flour, baking powder and salt in a medium bowl. Cut in butter until mixture resembles coarse crumbs. Make a well in centre.

Add water to well. Stir until a firm dough forms. Divide dough into 8 balls. Flatten each ball slightly with the palm of your hand and prick centre with a fork. Fry on low heat until golden, about 5 minutes, turning halfway through. Serve warm. Makes 8 cakes.

***1 cake:** 200 Calories; 10 g Total Fat (4.5 g Mono, 2 g Poly, 2.5 g Sat); 10 mg Cholesterol; 24 g Carbohydrate (trace Fibre, 0 g Sugar); 3 g Protein; 150 mg Sodium*

Before the 1960s, Canada did not see much immigration from the Caribbean, but in 1796, almost 550 Jamaican Maroons (escaped slaves who rebelled against British rule in Jamaica) were deported and shipped to Nova Scotia. They settled in Halifax, where they helped shore up Halifax's defences, building the Citadel and Government House, amongst other defense structures. Many of these settlers eventually relocated to Freetown in Sierra Leone.

Bannock

Bannock originated in Scotland and Northern England and was brought to Canada by the early fur traders and settlers. It soon became a staple of the native and pioneer diets, as they adapted what ingredients and baking methods were available at the time. Bannock can be pan-fried or baked in the oven, but it's much more fun to wrap the dough around a stick and cook it over a campfire. Be sure to whittle away the outer skin of your cooking stick to avoid the bitter taste of the bark.

All-purpose flour	**1 1/4 cups**	**300 mL**
Baking powder	**1 tbsp.**	**15 mL**
Salt	**1 tsp.**	**5 mL**
Sugar	**1 tbsp.**	**15 mL**
Butter (or hard margarine)	**3 tbsp.**	**45 mL**
Large egg	**1**	**1**
Water	**1/2 cup**	**125 mL**
Cooking oil	**1 tbsp.**	**15 mL**

Combine flour, baking powder, salt and sugar in a large bowl. Rub butter into flour mixture.

Combine egg and 1/4 cup (60 mL) water. Add to flour mixture, stirring to combine. Add enough of remaining water to make firm dough. Knead dough for about 3 minutes. Let dough stand, covered, for 30 minutes.

Divide dough into quarters and shape each portion into a ball. Flatten with a rolling pin, or your hand, into a disk about 1/2 inch (1 cm) thick. Heat a frying pan over medium and add oil. Cook bannock on both sides, turning once, until golden brown. Alternatively, forego frying pan and simply twist dough evenly around a clean stick and hold it over an open campfire until golden and crispy. Makes 4 bannock.

***1 bannock:** 250 Calories; 10 g Total Fat (2.5 g Mono, 0.5 g Poly, 6 g Sat); 75 mg Cholesterol; 34 g Carbohydrate (1 g Fibre, 3 g Sugar); 6 g Protein; 830 mg Sodium*

Why They Came...the Russians

The first Russians to come to Canada were fur traders that wandered south from Alaska into BC in the late 1700s. Emigration from Russia was restricted, so most of the early Russian immigrants to this country came in groups that were given special allowances by the Russian government. As a result, Russia did not have much of a presence in Canada before the 1870s.

The Mennonites were one of the earliest and largest groups of Russian immigrants. In the mid 19th century, Russia was undergoing a rather intense bout of Russification, in which all non-Russians in the empire were expected to adopt the Russian language and live by policies that promoted Russian culture. Much about Russification went against the tenets of the Mennonites' way of life; they were particularly distressed by the fact that they could no longer school their children in German and were expected to serve in the military, which went against their religious convictions. As a result, in the 1870s about 7000 Mennonites came to Canada, where they were promised land, religious freedom and conscientious objector status, meaning they would be exempt from military service. They settled in southern Manitoba. In the 1920s, about 20,000 Russian Mennonites fleeing the Bolshevik regime joined that community.

Also seeking religious freedom, in 1899 approximately 7500 Doukhobors (nearly a third of the population) left Russia and immigrated to Saskatchewan. They were joined in 1902 by another 500 individuals, including their spiritual leader, Peter Verigin. However, all was not well on the commune. Because they would not take an oath of allegiance to the Crown, the government revoked the titles for their homesteads. In protest, the majority of Doukhobors moved to BC in 1908, where they lived on a parcel of land bought by Verigin. Some of those who stayed in Saskatchewan decided to live independently and set up their own homesteads. Other, more extremist individuals formed a radical group known as the Freedomites or Sons of Freedom, who would also eventually move to BC, where they would become a thorn in the side of the BC government and shock the Canadian public with their nudist protests.

The late 1800s saw a few thousand Russian Jews arrive in Canada, escaping the pogroms and poverty of their homeland. They established small communities in Toronto, Montréal, Winnipeg, Vancouver and Victoria.

At the end of World War I, an estimated 1 million people left Russia, hundreds of thousands of them heading to Canada. Thousands more Russian people came after 1948, but the majority of them came from Europe, especially from Germany, having been displaced by World War II. They found jobs mostly as farm labourers or in resource extraction, though some were well educated and settled in urban centres.

Chebureki

Chebureki could be considered a Russian version of the empanada or panzarotti. Unleavened dough is folded over a mixture of minced meat, onions and vegetables, and then deep- or pan-fried to golden perfection. Chebureki can be eaten as either an appetizer or main dish and is a common street food in Russia and other former USSR nations. Because it is so portable, it makes a perfect lunch for the office or classroom. We've used ground beef in this recipe, but you could also use ground pork or lamb.

Water	**1 cup**	**250 mL**
Butter	**2 tbsp.**	**30 mL**
Salt	**1/2 tsp.**	**2 mL**
All-purpose flour	**1/2 cup**	**125 mL**
Egg, slightly beaten	**1**	**1**
All-purpose flour	**3 1/2 cup**	**875 mL**
Ground beef	**1 lb.**	**454 g**
Chopped onion	**1/4 cup**	**60 mL**
Chopped mushrooms	**1/4 cup**	**60 mL**
Spinach	**2 cups**	**500 mL**
Salt, to taste		
Pepper, to taste		
Cooking oil	**2 tbsp.**	**30 mL**

Bring water to a boil in a large pot. Add butter and salt, stirring until melted. Mix in 1/2 cup (125 mL) flour and stir until smooth.

Add egg and remaining 3 1/2 cups (875 mL) flour to make a dough, adding extra flour if needed. Knead dough until soft and smooth. Let rest in a covered bowl at room temperature for one hour.

Cook ground beef in a medium frying pan on medium until no longer pink inside. Add onion and mushrooms, and cook until soft. Add spinach, salt and pepper, and cook until spinach wilts. Set aside to cool.

Roll dough out into a thin sheet 1/8 inch (30 mm) thick and cut into 3 inch (7.5 cm) circles. Place heaping tablespoonful of filling on one side of the circle and fold over, pressing to seal.

Heat oil in a large pan over medium heat. Fry chebureki, a few at a time, until golden brown. Makes 24 chebureki.

1 chebureki: *140 Calories; 5 g Total Fat (2 g Mono, 0.5 g Poly, 2 g Sat); 25 mg Cholesterol; 16 g Carbohydrate (trace Fibre, 0 g Sugar); 6 g Protein; 70 mg Sodium*

Crumpets

Crumpets are thought to have originated in the 5th century with the Anglo-Saxons, but the soft, spongy version we are familiar with today was not seen until Victorian times. This humble bread was a favourite food of commoner and royalty alike. Then, as now, the crumpet was generally served toasted and slathered with butter (and sometimes jam), which pooled in its characteristic holey surface. In the UK, it is a mainstay of the British Afternoon Tea, but in Canada it is more common as a breakfast food.

All-purpose flour	**2 cups**	**500 mL**
White bread flour	**2 cups**	**500 mL**
Salt	**2 tsp.**	**10 mL**
Milk	**1 1/4 cups**	**300 mL**
Water	**1 1/4 cups**	**300 mL**
Sunflower oil	**2 tbsp.**	**30 mL**
Superfine sugar	**1 tbsp.**	**15 mL**
1/4 oz. (7 g) package of active dry yeast	**1**	**1**
Lukewarm water	**1/2 cup**	**125 mL**
Baking soda	**1/2 tsp.**	**2 mL**

Combine both flours and salt in a large mixing bowl and make a well in centre.

Combine milk, water, oil and sugar in a small pot and heat until lukewarm. Sprinkle yeast over top. Let stand for 10 minutes. Stir to dissolve yeast.

Pour yeast mixture into well in flour mixture and beat firmly for 5 minutes until batter is smooth and elastic. Cover with greased plastic wrap and let stand in oven with light on and door closed until mixture is bubbly, about 1 1/2 hours.

Combine lukewarm water and soda in a small bowl. Stir to dissolve soda and then stir into batter. Cover with greased plastic wrap and let stand in oven with light on and door closed for 30 minutes. Heat 4 greased 3 inch (7.5 cm) crumpet rings or round cookie cutters in a greased heavy-bottomed frying pan over medium. Fill rings about 1/2 inch (12 mm) deep and cook for about 6 minutes until small holes cover tops and batter has dried. Carefully remove rings before turning crumpets over. Cook for another 1 to 2 minutes until lightly golden. Repeat with remaining batter. Makes 20 crumpets.

1 crumpet: *120 Calories; 2 g Total Fat (0 g Mono, 1 g Poly, 0 g Sat); 0 mg Cholesterol; 21 g Carbohydrate (trace Fibre, 2 g Sugar); 4 g Protein; 280 mg Sodium*

Irish Soda Bread

Irish soda bread is the traditional bread of Ireland. Classic soda bread was made with four simple ingredients—flour, salt, baking soda and buttermilk. The dough was shaped into a circle and either marked with the sign of a cross or cut into quarters, known as farls, before being baked in a Dutch oven or on a griddle. In a country where many people lived in extreme poverty, soda bread went a long way to staving off starvation. This bread would have served Irish immigrants to Canada well, too, during the lean years that often followed settling in a new country. We've included a dressed-up version of soda bread here, which contains egg, sugar and butter, ingredients that would have been too expensive for many Irish families, both in their homeland and arriving in Canada. A similar version known as "spotted dog" in Ireland contains raisins.

Buttermilk	**1 1/2 cups**	**375 mL**
Butter (or hard margarine), melted	**2 tbsp.**	**30 mL**
Egg, lightly beaten	**1**	**1**
Seedless raisins or currants (optional)	**1 1/2 cups**	**375 mL**
All-purpose flour	**3 cups**	**750 mL**
Sugar	**2/3 cup**	**150 mL**
Baking powder	**1 tbsp.**	**15 mL**
Baking soda	**1 tsp.**	**5 mL**
Salt	**1 tsp.**	**5 mL**

Combine buttermilk, butter, egg and raisins, if using, in a medium bowl.

Combine remaining 5 ingredients in a large bowl and mix thoroughly. Make a well in centre. Add buttermilk mixture to dry ingredients and mix until combined. Spoon into greased 9 inch (23 cm) round pan. Bake in 350°F (175°C) oven for about 45 minutes. Test for doneness by rapping the loaf with your knuckles—it should sound hollow. Let stand in pan for 1 minute, then remove and transfer to a wire rack to cool. Makes 1 loaf. Cuts into 4 farls.

1/2 farl: *390 Calories; 4.5 g Total Fat (1 g Mono, 0 g Poly, 2 g Sat); 40 mg Cholesterol; 78 g Carbohydrate (3 g Fibre, 39 g Sugar); 6 g Protein; 610 mg Sodium*

Soda bread is usually baked daily because it goes stale quickly.

Scottish Oatcakes

Now widely considered to be "the bread of Scotland," the oatcake's humble beginnings go back at least as far as 14th century to the Highlands of Scotland. Soldiers on the move carried small sacks of oats, which they would mix with water and form into cakes. To cook the oatcakes, the men would heat their sheilds over a campfire and use them as hot plates. Through the ages, this basic survival food was adopted throughout Scotland, with every region fine-tuning the cakes to suit their tastes. Scottish immigrants to the New World brought their recipes to the Maritimes and beyond. Traditionally included as part of most meals, oatcakes are now generally served alongside crackers with a cheese tray or eaten spread with butter or jam as a light breakfast or snack.

Medium or fine oatmeal	**1 cup**	**250 mL**
Salt	**1/4 tsp.**	**1 mL**
Baking soda	**1/4 tsp.**	**1 mL**
Butter, melted	**1 tbsp.**	**15 mL**
Hot water	**3 tsp.**	**45 mL**

In a medium bowl, combine oatmeal, salt and baking soda.

Add melted butter and enough hot water to form a dough. Turn out onto a surface dusted with oatmeal and knead until smooth. Roll out into a very thin 12 x 8 inch (30 x 20 cm) rectangle about 1/4 inch (6 mm) thick. Cut out oatcakes with a 2 inch (5 cm) cookie cutter. Heat a lightly oiled frying pan over medium. Cook over low heat for 2 to 3 minutes. Use a spatula to turn over and cook another 1 to 2 minutes. Transfer to a wire rack to cool. Oatcakes can also be cooked in 350°F (175°C) oven for about 13 to 15 minutes. Makes 24 oatcakes.

1 oatcake: *15 Calories; 0.5 g Total Fat (trace Mono, 0 g Poly, trace Sat); trace Cholesterol; 2 g Carbohydrate (trace Fibre, 0 g Sugar); trace Protein; 40 mg Sodium*

Scones

Scones most likely originated in the British Isles, with England, Scotland and Ireland all claiming them as their own invention. In the UK, they are a big part of afternoon or Devonshire tea, where they are served slathered with jam and clotted cream. In Canada, we tend to use the terms "scone," "tea biscuit" and "biscuit" interchangeably. Biscuits were a staple during Canada's cowboy era, and a camp or chuckwagon cook would be forgiven for many culinary blunders as long as his biscuits were good.

All-purpose flour	**2 cups**	**500 mL**
Baking powder	**2 tsp.**	**10 mL**
Baking soda	**1/2 tsp.**	**2 mL**
Salt	**1/2 tsp.**	**2 mL**
Cold butter (or hard margarine), cut up	**1/4 cup**	**60 mL**
Buttermilk	**3/4 cup**	**175 mL**

Combine first 4 ingredients in a large bowl. Cut in butter until mixture resembles coarse crumbs. Make a well in centre.

Add buttermilk to well. Stir until a soft dough forms. Turn out onto a lightly floured surface. Knead 8 times. Roll or pat out to 1/2 inch (12 mm) thickness. Cut out into circles with a lightly floured 2 inch (5 cm) biscuit cutter. Arrange about 1 inch (2.5 cm) apart on a greased baking sheet. Bake in 400°F (200°C) oven for about 15 minutes until golden. Let stand on baking sheet for 5 minutes before removing to wire rack. Makes 18 scones.

***1 scone:** 80 Calories; 3 g Total Fat (0.5 g Mono, 0 g Poly, 1.5 g Sat); 10 mg Cholesterol; 11 g Carbohydrate (0 g Fibre, 0 g Sugar); 1 g Protein; 140 mg Sodium*

Keks

Classic keks is a moist tea cake found traditionally in most Russian households since the last century, and every home has its own variation. It is an ideal bread to pair with a cup of tea or coffee in the morning. We've used raisins in this recipe, but 1/2 cup (125 mL) dried cranberries or chopped dried apricots and 1 tsp. (5 mL) orange zest added to the dough would also be delicious.

Butter, at room temperature	**2/3 cup**	**150 mL**
Sugar	**3/4 cup**	**175 mL**
Large eggs	**3**	**3**
Vanilla extract	**1 tsp.**	**5 mL**
Salt	**1/2 tsp.**	**2 mL**
All-purpose flour	**1 cup**	**250 mL**
Baking powder	**3/4 tsp.**	**4 mL**
Raisins	**3/4 cup**	**175 mL**
Powdered sugar	**1 tbsp.**	**15 mL**

Beat butter and sugar in a large mixing bowl until light and fluffy.

Add eggs, one at a time, mixing continuously. Add vanilla and salt.

Combine flour and baking powder in a separate bowl. Stir in raisins. Add butter mixture and mix thoroughly. Fill 6 greased 4 1/2 × 2 1/2 inch (11 x 6.5 cm) mini loaf pans 2/3 full. Bake in 325°F (160°C) oven for 45 to 50 minutes. Remove from oven and dust with powdered sugar. Transfer to a wire rack to cool. Makes 6 mini loaves.

1 mini loaf: *450 Calories; 23 g Total Fat (6 g Mono, 1.5 g Poly, 3.5 g Sat); 15 mg Cholesterol; 22 g Carbohydrate (0 g Fibre, 9 g Sugar); 2 g Protein; 125 mg Sodium*

Cinnamon Buns

Although cinnamon buns have been attributed to as far back as Ancient Greece, the buns as we know them today most likely originated in Europe in the mid-1700s. As proof, look to Germany's schneken *and Sweden's* kanelbulle, *which although somewhat different than the Canadian cinnamon bun could have served as prototypes. For a truly Canadian experience, try a Persian bun, a deep-fried cinnamon bun/donut cross that is spread with pink icing and is a specialty of Thunder Bay. Whether the pink icing should be strawberry or raspberry is apparently a matter of contention amongst the locals.*

Sugar	**1/2 cup**	**125 mL**
Warm water	**3 cups**	**750 mL**
1/4 oz. (7 g) package of active dry yeast	**2**	**2**
Large eggs	**2**	**2**
Cooking oil	**1/2 cup**	**125 mL**
Salt	**1 tsp.**	**5 mL**
All-purpose flour	**9 cups**	**2.25 L**
Brown sugar, packed	**1 cup**	**250 mL**
Ground cinnamon	**1 tbsp.**	**15 mL**
Butter (or hard margarine), softened	**3/4 cup**	**175 mL**
Icing (confectioner's) sugar	**1 1/2 cups**	**375 mL**
Milk	**1/4 cup**	**60 mL**
Vanilla	**1/2 tsp.**	**2 mL**

Stir sugar in warm water in a large bowl. Sprinkle yeast over top. Let stand 10 minutes. Stir to dissolve yeast.

Mix in eggs, cooking oil and salt. Work in enough flour until dough pulls away from sides of bowl. Turn out onto floured surface. Knead 8 to 10 minutes until smooth and elastic. Divide dough into 4 equal parts. Roll 1 part at a time 1/4 inch (6 mm) thick into 9 x 12 inch (23 x 30 cm) rectangle.

Combine brown sugar and cinnamon in a small bowl. Spread each rectangle with 2 tbsp. (30 mL) butter and sprinkle 1/4 cup (60 mL) brown sugar mixture over top. Roll each rectangle up from long side. Cut into 1 inch (2.5 cm) slices. Place cut side down in greased 9 x 13 inch (23 x 33 cm) pan 1/4 inch (6 mm) apart. Cover with tea towel. Let stand in oven with light on and door closed for about 1 hour until doubled in size. Bake in 375°F (190°C) oven for about 20 minutes. Turn out right side up on rack.

Beat icing sugar, milk and vanilla together in a bowl adding more icing sugar or milk to make a thin glaze. Spoon over warm buns. Makes 48 buns.

1 bun: *170 Calories; 6 g Total Fat (2 g Mono, 1 g Poly, 2 g Sat); 15 mg Cholesterol; 28 g Carbohydrate (trace Fibre, 10 g Sugar); 3 g Protein; 55 mg Sodium*

Why They Came...the English, Scottish and Irish

For generations John Cabot was credited as the first European to reach Canada (though the Vikings beat him by at least 400 years), and he helped open the door to European exploration of this country. While travelling under the commission of King Henry VII in 1497, Cabot reached landfall on the east coast of what is now Canada, landing most likely in Newfoundland, Labrador or Cape Breton and claiming the area for England. His accounts of waters bursting with cod inspired other European nations, particularly Spain and Portugal, to venture to capitalize on the excellent fishing off Newfoundland's coast.

The fur trade in the vast interior of the continent came to the attention of Prince Rupert, cousin to King Charles II, and the Hudson's Bay Company was granted a royal charter to Rupert's Land in 1670. Despite Cabot's early claim to North America and numerous explorations and fur-trading activities into the interior, the British did not have much presence here in Canada until Britain took over New France in 1763. Even after that, Britain did not promote immigration to Canada; they didn't believe the influx of English-speaking Protestants would much improve the situation with a resentful population of French-speaking Catholics in the former colony of New France.

However, things changed with the Clearances in Scotland. One of the largest ethnic groups in Canada, and one of the first to settle here, Scottish immigrants had been trickling into Canada as early as the 1620s, but migration took off in the 1770s when Highland farmers were driven from their farms. Between 1815 and 1870, Canada saw an even larger influx or Scots as the Lowland Clearances took place and even more Scots were left homeless and destitute. The British government encouraged the evicted families to relocate to Canada, with their former landlords paying their passage.

In England, the Industrial Revolution caused a decrease in the number of jobs as the population of England was increasing, and cities were becoming overcrowded with people who had little or no means to support themselves. Again, the British government saw emigration as a solution and encouraged its citizens to relocate to Canada.

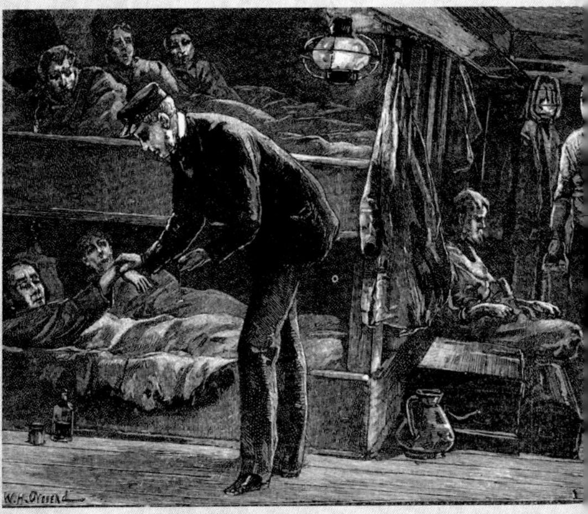

And then there were the Irish. Canada began to receive a large number of Irish immigrants in the early 1700s, when ships transporting timber from Canada to England for the English Navy's shipbuilding endeavours didn't want to make the return trip with empty hulls, so the British government offered cheap transportation to Irish people willing to settle in North America. The majority of Irish immigrants, however, came to Canada during the Great Potato Famine of the 1840s, when the repeated failure of potato crops caused unimaginable suffering in Ireland. More than 1 million people died of starvation and resulting disease, and an additional 1 million people left Ireland, hoping for better fortune abroad. People who decided to relocate to Canada crossed the Atlantic in "coffin ships," so called because conditions onboard were so bad that many people died along the way. When the ships made it to harbour, they were quarantined until the people could be checked for communicable diseases, particularly typhus, which was rampant on the ships. Thousands of Irish immigrants died in quarantine.

Despite the circumstances in which many of them left their homeland and came to Canada, people of Scotland, Ireland and England went on to have an enormous influence in the shaping of our country. We also have them to thank for many of our food traditions and, of course, our breads.

Chelsea Buns

Chelsea buns are a wonderful hybrid of cinnamon rolls and fruit cake. The traditional British-style Chelsea bun, invented in London around 1700 at the Old Chelsea Bun House, is covered with a sticky glaze and studded with currants. It was often sold alongside hot cross buns on Good Friday but was available all other times of the year as well. These sweet buns crossed economic barriers in England, being just as popular with royalty as with the working class. Today the same kind of Chelsea bun can be found in bakeries and farmers' markets all over cottage country in the central Ontario regions of Muskoka, Haliburton and Kawartha Lakes.

Milk	**1 cup**	**250 mL**
Large egg	**1**	**1**
White bread flour	**4 1/2 cups**	**1.1 L**
Salt	**1/2 tsp.**	**2 mL**
Superfine sugar	**6 tbsp.**	**90 mL**
Butter, softened	**1/4 cup**	**60 mL**
Instant yeast	**1 tsp.**	**5 mL**
Melted butter	**2 tbsp.**	**30 mL**
Sultana raisins	**2/3 cup**	**160 mL**
Mixed chopped candied peel	**3 tbsp.**	**45 mL**
Currants	**2 tbsp.**	**30 mL**
Brown sugar	**2 tbsp.**	**30 mL**
Ground cinnamon	**1/4 tsp.**	**1 mL**
Ground cloves	**1/4 tsp.**	**1 mL**
Ground nutmeg	**1/4 tsp.**	**1 mL**
Ground ginger	**1/4 tsp.**	**1 mL**
Superfine sugar	**1/4 cup**	**60 mL**
Water	**1/4 cup**	**60 mL**
Orange blossom water	**1 tsp.**	**5 mL**

Pour milk into a bread machine pan. Add egg. Sprinkle flour over top, completely covering liquid. Place salt, first amount of sugar and softened butter in separate corners of bread machine pan. Make a well in centre of flour and add yeast. Start dough cycle according to your machine's instructions.

Once dough cycle has completed, place dough on a lightly floured surface. Punch dough down gently and roll out to form a 12 inch (30 cm) square. Brush with melted butter and sprinkle sultanas, peel, currants, brown sugar and spices evenly over top, leaving a 1/3 inch (1 cm) border along one edge. Starting with covered edge, roll dough up like a jelly roll and seal

(continued on next page)

by pressing edges together. Cut into 12 even slices and place cut side up in a greased 9 inch (23 cm) square pan. Cover with a piece of oiled plastic wrap and let stand in oven with light on and door closed for 30 to 45 minutes until doubled in size. Bake in 400°F (200°C) oven for 15 to 20 minutes, until buns have risen and are golden. Let stand in pan to cool slightly, then transfer to a rack to finish cooling.

For the glaze, mix remaining superfine sugar with water in a small pan. Heat on low, stirring, until sugar dissolves. Increase heat and boil mix for 1 to 2 minutes, without stirring, until syrupy. Stir in orange blossom water. Remove from heat and brush over warm buns. Makes 12 buns.

***1 bun:** 350 Calories; 7 g Total Fat (1.5 g Mono, 0.5 g Poly, 4 g Sat); 35 mg Cholesterol; 62 g Carbohydrate (2 g Fibre, 22 g Sugar); 8 g Protein; 120 mg Sodium*

Pets de Soeur

It was Samuel de Champlain who brought the Roman Catholic Church to New France. The French clergy and aristocracy supported the establishment of various orders, including the Jesuits, to create schools and hospitals in the St. Lawrence Valley and beyond. In the early days of the French Canadian habitants, the Catholic Church formed the backbone of the community, providing structure and support; the church was also a strong, overbearing and often-feared influence. This situation created somewhat of a love-hate relationship between the church and the parishioners, and many derogatory phrases sprang from this time. Thankfully, these little cinnamon pastries taste nothing like their name; pets de soeur *literally translates as "nun's farts." They will keep for up to 2 weeks in a sealed container.*

All-purpose flour	**3 cups**	**750 mL**
Baking powder	**2 tsp.**	**10 mL**
Sea salt	**1 tsp.**	**5 mL**
Chilled butter	**1/2 cup**	**125 mL**
Milk	**1 cup**	**250 mL**
Butter, softened	**1/4 cup**	**60 mL**
Brown sugar	**1 cup**	**250 mL**
Ground cinnamon	**1 tsp.**	**5 mL**

Combine first 3 ingredients in a large bowl. Using a fork, cut in butter until mixture resembles coarse meal. Stir in milk to form a dough. Cover and let rest for 15 minutes.

Roll dough out as thin as you would for a pie crust. Spread dough with softened butter and sprinkle evenly with brown sugar and cinnamon. Roll dough up like a jelly roll and cut into 1/4 inch (0.5 cm) slices. Bake in 375°F (175°C) oven for 15 to 20 minutes or until golden brown. Makes 24 pastries.

1 pastry: *150 Calories; 6 g Total Fat (1.5 g Mono, 0 g Poly, 3.5 g Sat); 15 mg Cholesterol; 22 g Carbohydrate (0 g Fibre, 9 g Sugar); 2 g Protein; 125 mg Sodium*

Pulla

The earliest Finns to immigrate to Canada made their way to southern BC via Alaska in the 1800s. Like the Chinese, the Finns are famed for their work on the Canadian Pacific Railway, and they also found employment in the timber trade, in Ontario's mines and on the construction of the Welland Canal. Today, Thunder Bay boasts one of the largest Finnish communities outside of Finland. Finns here and in Finland consume more coffee per capita than almost any other nationality. Pulla, a sweet coffee bread, is a popular Finnish recipe and a perfect match for a hot cup of joe. This bread is best when served the same day, and it is even more delicious served oven fresh. Day-old pulla is excellent for toast, bread pudding and French toast.

Milk	**3/4 cup**	**175 mL**
Brown sugar	**1/2 cup**	**125 mL**
Butter	**1/3 cup**	**75 mL**
Sugar	**1 tsp.**	**5 mL**
Warm water	**1/4 cup**	**60 mL**
1/4 oz. (7 g) package of active dry yeast	**1**	**1**
Large eggs, beaten	**2**	**2**
Ground cardamom	**1/2 tsp.**	**2 mL**
Sea salt	**1 tsp.**	**5 mL**
Whole wheat flour	**1 cup**	**250 mL**
All-purpose flour	**4 cups**	**1 L**
Coffee	**1 tbsp.**	**15 mL**
Milk	**1 tbsp.**	**15 mL**
Large egg, beaten	**1**	**1**
Turbinado sugar	**1/3 cup**	**75 mL**

Scald first amount of milk in a pot; remove from heat and stir in brown sugar and butter. Set aside to cool to lukewarm.

Stir sugar into warm water in a small bowl. Sprinkle yeast over top. Let stand 10 minutes. Stir to dissolve yeast.

Stir first amount of eggs, cardamom, yeast mixture and salt into milk mixture. Beat in whole wheat flour and 1 cup (250 mL) of all-purpose flour. Continue adding flour, 1/2 cup (125 mL) at a time, until you have medium-firm dough. Turn dough out onto a lightly floured surface and knead dough for 10 minutes, adding flour if dough is sticky.

Place dough in a large greased bowl, turning once to coat top. Cover with plastic wrap and a tea towel and let stand in oven with light on and door closed until doubled, about 1 1/2 hours. Punch down, and divide dough

(continued on next page)

into thirds. Roll each piece into a strand 18 inches (45 cm) long. Braid strands into a loaf and place on a greased baking sheet. Let stand, covered, in oven with light on and door closed until almost doubled, about 40 minutes.

Combine coffee and remaining milk and egg in a bowl. Brush over loaf and sprinkle with turbinado sugar. Bake in 375°F (190°C) oven for 30 to 35 minutes, until golden and bread springs back when pressed firmly. Transfer to a wire rack to cool. Makes 1 loaf. Cuts into 20 slices.

***1 slice:** 110 Calories; 0 g Total Fat (0 g Mono, 0 g Poly, 0 g Sat); 0 mg Cholesterol; 26 g Carbohydrate (2 g Fibre, 10 g Sugar); 2 g Protein; 200 mg Sodium*

Doughnuts

Although breads made of deep-fried dough are found worldwide, with different cultures having their own variations, doughnuts as we know them today originated in the U.S. When early Dutch settlers arrived in America, they brought with them their traditional olykoeks ("oily cakes,") deep-fried balls of dough that often had a fruit or nut filling to make up for the fact that the centre didn't cook through. As the story goes, a ship captain named Hanson Gregory disliked the filling in his mother's olykoeks so he pushed the centre out. His next step was to create a centre-less (i.e., ring-shaped) olykoek, and so the doughnut was born. It may be an American invention, but Canadians have made it their own. We have more doughnut shops and eat more doughnuts per capita than any other country, thanks largely to the Tim Hortons franchise, founded in 1964 in Hamilton by NHL defenceman Tim Horton. With this recipe, try frying up the doughnut holes, too, to make your own homemade "Timbits."

Butter (or hard margarine)	**1 1/2 tbsp.**	**22 mL**
Salt	**1 1/2 tsp.**	**7 mL**
Ground nutmeg	**1 tsp.**	**5 mL**
Sugar	**1/4 cup**	**60 mL**
Milk, scalded	**3/4 cup**	**(175 mL**
Large egg, beaten	**1**	**1**
Sugar	**1 tsp.**	**5 mL**
Warm water	**1/4 cup**	**60 mL**
1/4 oz. (7 g) package of active dry yeast	**1**	**1**
All-purpose flour	**3 1/4 cups**	**800 mL**
Cooking oil	**3 cups**	**750 mL**
Sugar	**1 cup**	**250 mL**

Combine butter, salt, nutmeg and first amount of sugar in a large bowl. Stir in scalded milk. Cool to lukewarm.

Mix in beaten egg.

Stir remaining sugar in warm water in a small bowl. Sprinkle yeast over top. Let stand 10 minutes. Stir to dissolve yeast. Add to batter.

Work in enough flour until dough pulls away from sides of bowl. Turn out onto a floured surface. Knead 8 to 10 minutes until smooth and elastic. Place in a greased bowl, turning once to grease top. Cover with a tea towel. Let stand in oven with light on and door closed for about 1 1/2 hours until doubled in size. Punch dough down. Cover with a tea towel. Let stand in oven with light on and door closed for 30 minutes. Roll out 1/2 inch

(continued on next page)

(12 mm) thick on lightly floured board. Cut with a doughnut cutter. Cover with a tea towel. Let stand in oven with light on and door closed for about 1 hour until doubled in size.

Deep-fry in hot 375°F (190°C) fat, placing raised side (top side) down until brown. Turn to brown other side. Drain on paper towels.

Sprinkle with sugar while hot, if desired. Makes 18 doughnuts.

1 doughnut: *190 Calories; 8 g Total Fat (4 g Mono, 2 g Poly, 1.5 g Sat); 15 mg Cholesterol; 27 g Carbohydrate (trace Fibre, 10 g Sugar); 3 g Protein; 210 mg Sodium*

Tim Hortons set up shop on a Canadian military base in Kandahar from 2006–11 to provide a taste of home to troops deployed in Afghanistan. They even had their own version of the Roll Up the Rim to Win contest.

Butterhorns

The history of this tasty little bread is quite murky, but anyone growing up in Alberta in the '50s or '60s will have fond memories of the butterhorn. Not to be confused with the cresent-shaped pastry of the same name, which looks much like a small croissant or Jewish rugelach, this butterhorn more closely resembles a Danish. At one time, you could buy them from local bakeries, and toasted butterhorns slathered with butter were a common offering at roadside cafes throughout the province, but they are no longer so easy to find.

Milk	**2 cups**	**500 mL**
Salt	**1 tsp.**	**5 mL**
Sugar	**1/2 cup**	**125 mL**
Butter (or hard margarine), softened	**1 cup**	**250 mL**
Sugar	**1 tsp.**	**5 mL**
Warm water	**1/2 cup**	**125 mL**
1/4 oz. (7 g) package of active dry yeast	**1**	**1**
All-purpose flour	**6 cups**	**1.5 L**
Large egg, beaten	**1**	**1**
Icing (confectioner's) sugar	**2 cups**	**500 mL**
Butter (or hard margarine), softened	**3 tbsp.**	**45 mL**
Milk	**2 tbsp.**	**30 mL**
Vanilla	**1 tsp.**	**5 mL**
Shaved almonds or finely chopped walnuts	**1/2 cup**	**125 mL**

Scald milk in saucepan. Remove from heat. Add salt and first amounts of sugar and butter. Stir to dissolve sugar and melt butter. Cool to lukewarm.

Stir remaining sugar in warm water in a small bowl. Sprinkle yeast over top. Let stand 10 minutes. Stir to dissolve yeast.

Measure flour into a large bowl. Make a well in centre. Pour egg into well. Add yeast mixture and milk mixture. Mix with a spoon to moisten. Beat with spoon until mixed well. Cover with greased waxed paper and a tea towel. Let stand in oven with light on and door closed for about 1 hour until doubled in size. Gently stir down with a spoon. Cover with greased waxed paper and tea towel. Let stand in oven with light on and door closed for about 30 minutes until doubled in size. Stir dough down. Divide dough into 2 portions. Roll out one portion on floured surface to 10 x 12 inch (25 x 30 cm) rectangle. Cut into 12 strips. Take each strip and roll lightly to smooth sides. Beginning with one end being the centre, coil rest of strip around it. Pinch end to side of coil. Repeat with other portions. Place 2 inches (5 cm) apart on greased baking sheet. Cover with greased waxed

(continued on next page)

paper and tea towel. Let stand in oven with light on and door closed for about 30 minutes until doubled in size. Bake in 375°F (190°C) oven for about 20 minutes. Place on racks to cool.

Mix next 4 ingredients together well, adding more icing sugar or milk for proper spreading consistency. Spread or dizzle icing over butterhorns and sprinkle with nuts. Makes 24 butterhorns.

***1 butterhorn:** 280 Calories; 12 g Total Fat (3.5 g Mono, 1 g Poly, 7 g Sat); 40 mg Cholesterol; 38 g Carbohydrate (1 g Fibre, 14 g Sugar); 5 g Protein; 115 mg Sodium*

Bara Brith

When people first arrived in Canada from Wales is a matter of some dispute. Welsh folklore tells of a Welsh prince, Madoc, sailing to North America in the 1170s and landing in Newfoundland or Nova Scotia, but this tale has largely been discredited. There has, however, been a slow but steady stream of Welsh immigration to Canada, with some people drawn by the Cariboo Gold Rush in BC, some settling in as farmers in Saskatchewan and Ontario, and others drawn to the coal mines of Alberta. Bara Brith is a traditional Welsh bread and is one of best-known fruit breads from the UK. Historically it was made with only currants, but raisins and candied fruits are now included in most recipes.

All-purpose flour	**1 cup**	**250 mL**
Sugar	**1/2 cup**	**125 mL**
Salt	**1 1/2 tsp.**	**7 mL**
Grated lemon peel	**1 tsp.**	**5 mL**
1/4 oz. (7 g) packages of active dry yeast	**3**	**3**
Water	**1 1/4 cups**	**300 mL**
Milk	**1/2 cup**	**125 mL**
Margarine	**1/4 cup**	**60 mL**
Eggs, room temperature	**2**	**2**
All-purpose flour	**4 1/2 cups**	**1.1 L**
Raisins	**1 cup**	**250 mL**
Currants	**1/4 cup**	**60 mL**
Chopped mixed candied fruits	**1/3 cup**	**75 mL**
Honey	**2 tbsp.**	**30 mL**

In a large bowl, combine first amount of flour, sugar, salt, lemon peel and undissolved yeast.

Combine water, milk and margarine in a saucepan. Heat over low heat until liquid is hot to touch. Gradually add to dry ingredients and beat 2 minutes with an electric mixer at medium speed or vigorously with a wooden spoon, scraping bowl occasionally.

Add eggs and 1/2 cup (125 mL) flour, enough to make a thick batter. Beat at medium speed for 1 minute. With a wooden spoon, stir in enough additional flour to make a soft dough. Add raisins, currants and mixed fruits and mix them in by hand. Turn dough out onto a lightly floured surface. Knead until smooth and elastic, about 8 to 10 minutes. Place in a greased bowl, turning once to grease top. Cover and let stand in oven with light on and door closed until doubled in size, about 60 minutes. Punch dough down and turn out onto a lightly floured surface. Divide in half and shape into loaves. Place into greased 9 x 5 x 3 inch (23 x 12.5 x 7.5 cm) loaf pans.

(continued on next page)

Cover and let stand in oven with light on and door closed until doubled in size or until dough is 1 inch (2.5 cm) above side of pan, about 50 minutes. Bake in 375°F (190°C) oven for 30 to 35 minutes. If loaves are browning too quickly, cover with foil. Brush top of warm loaves with honey and transfer to wire racks to cool. Makes 2 loaves. Each loaf cuts into 16 slices.

1 slice: *130 Calories; 2 g Total Fat (1 g Mono, 0.5 g Poly, 0 g Sat); 15 mg Cholesterol; 25 g Carbohydrate (1 g Fibre, 10 g Sugar); 3 g Protein; 135 mg Sodium*

Zwieback

Zwieback is a German crispbread whose popularity has spread beyond Germany's borders and into Austria, Denmark, Sweden and Norway. Light, crunchy and slightly sweet, zweiback was originally given to teething babies and people with stomach ailments, but before long it became a common snack for adults, too. The characteristic crispy texture comes from the dual baking process (the name means "twice baked" in German). The loaves are baked and allowed to stand uncovered overnight before being cut into slices, which are splayed out on baking sheets and baked again.

All-purpose flour	**4 cups**	**1 L**
Sugar	**6 tbsp.**	**90 mL**
Instant yeast	**2 1/2 tsp.**	**12 mL**
Salt	**1 1/4 tsp.**	**6 mL**
Ground cinnamon	**1/2 tsp.**	**2 mL**
Ground nutmeg	**1/4 tsp.**	**1 mL**
Butter, softened	**1/4 cup**	**60 mL**
Large egg	**1**	**1**
Lukewarm milk	**1 cup**	**250 mL**
Sugar	**1/4 cup**	**60 mL**
Ground cinnamon	**1 tsp.**	**5 mL**

Combine flour, first amount of sugar, yeast, salt, first amount of cinnamon and nutmeg in a large mixing bowl. Add butter, egg and milk, and knead to form a soft, slightly sticky dough. Cover with plastic wrap and let stand in oven with light on and door closed for about 2 hours. Cut dough in half and shape each piece into a 12 inch (30 cm) log. Place logs on a baking sheet lined with parchment paper. Cover with plastic wrap and let rise for about 90 minutes. Bake logs in 350°F (175°C) oven for 22 to 24 minutes, until golden brown. Remove bread from oven and transfer to a wire rack to cool. Let stand, uncovered, at room temperature overnight.

Combine remaining sugar and cinnamon in a small bowl. Set aside. Cut loaves into 1/2 inch (12 mm) slices and place on baking sheets lined with parchment paper. Bake in 200°F (95°C) oven for 1 hour. Remove from oven and sprinkle each toast with cinnamon sugar. Turn toasts over and bake for 1 hour. Transfer toasts to wire rack to cool. Makes 48 toasts.

***1 toast:** 60 Calories; 1 g Total Fat (0 g Mono, 0 g Poly, 0.5 g Sat); 5 mg Cholesterol; 12 g Carbohydrate (0 g Fibre, 4 g Sugar); 1 g Protein; 65 mg Sodium*

Beaver Tails

Beaver tails are a true Canadian success story. For those not in the know, a beaver tail is dough that has been hand stretched into the shape of a beaver's tail, then deep-fried and traditionally sprinkled with cinnamon sugar. Grant and Pamela Hooker first started selling these treats, made from a recipe that was handed down from Grant's grandmother, at their community fair in Killaloe in the late 1970s. In 1980, they opened their first stand in Ottawa's ByWard Market. Business was brisk enough to allow for a second location, opened the following year by the Rideau Canal Skateway. Today, the BeaverTail franchise has locations from BC to PEI and a few international stores, as well. Beaver tails gained international fame in 2009 when Barrack Obama picked one up at the ByWard Market location on his visit to Ottawa.

Sugar	**1 tsp.**	**15 mL**
Warm water	**1/2 cup**	**125 mL**
Active dry yeast	**1 1/2 tbsp.**	**22 mL**
Sugar	**1/3 cup**	**75 mL**
Warm milk	**1 cup**	**250 mL**
Vanilla	**1 tsp.**	**5 mL**
Large eggs	**2**	**2**
Oil	**1/3 cup**	**75 mL**
Salt	**1 tbsp.**	**15 mL**
Baking soda	**5 tsp.**	**25 mL**
All-purpose flour	**5 cups**	**1.25 L**
Vegetable oil	**3 cups**	**750 mL**
Cinnamon sugar	**2 tbsp.**	**30 mL**
Sugar	**1/3 cup**	**75 mL**

Stir first amount of sugar into warm water in a large bowl. Sprinkle yeast over top. Let stand 10 minutes. Stir to dissolve yeast.

Add second amount of sugar, milk, vanilla, eggs, oil, salt, baking soda and 4 1/2 cups (1.1 L) flour. Stir to form a soft dough. Knead 5 to 8 minutes, adding remaining flour as needed until a firm, smooth, elastic dough has formed. Place dough in a greased bowl, turning once to coat top and cover with plastic wrap. Let stand in oven with light on and door closed for 30 to 40 minutes. Gently punch down dough. Break off golf ball–sized pieces and roll into ovals. Shape each oval into a 5 inch (12 cm) beaver-tail shape, keeping rest of dough pieces covered with plastic wrap to prevent drying.

Heat oil in a fryer or wok to 350°F (175°C). Add dough pieces 1 or 2 at a time. Watch them carefully, turn when deep brown and remove with tongs to drain on paper towels.

(continued on next page)

Combine cinnamon and remaining sugar in a large shallow dish. Toss hot pastries with cinnamon sugar and shake off excess. Makes 25 beaver tails.

1 beaver tail: *180 Calories; 7 g Total Fat (3.5 g Mono, 1.5 g Poly, 0.5 g Sat); 15 mg Cholesterol; 27 g Carbohydrate (1 g Fibre, 7 g Sugar); 4 g Protein; 470 mg Sodium*

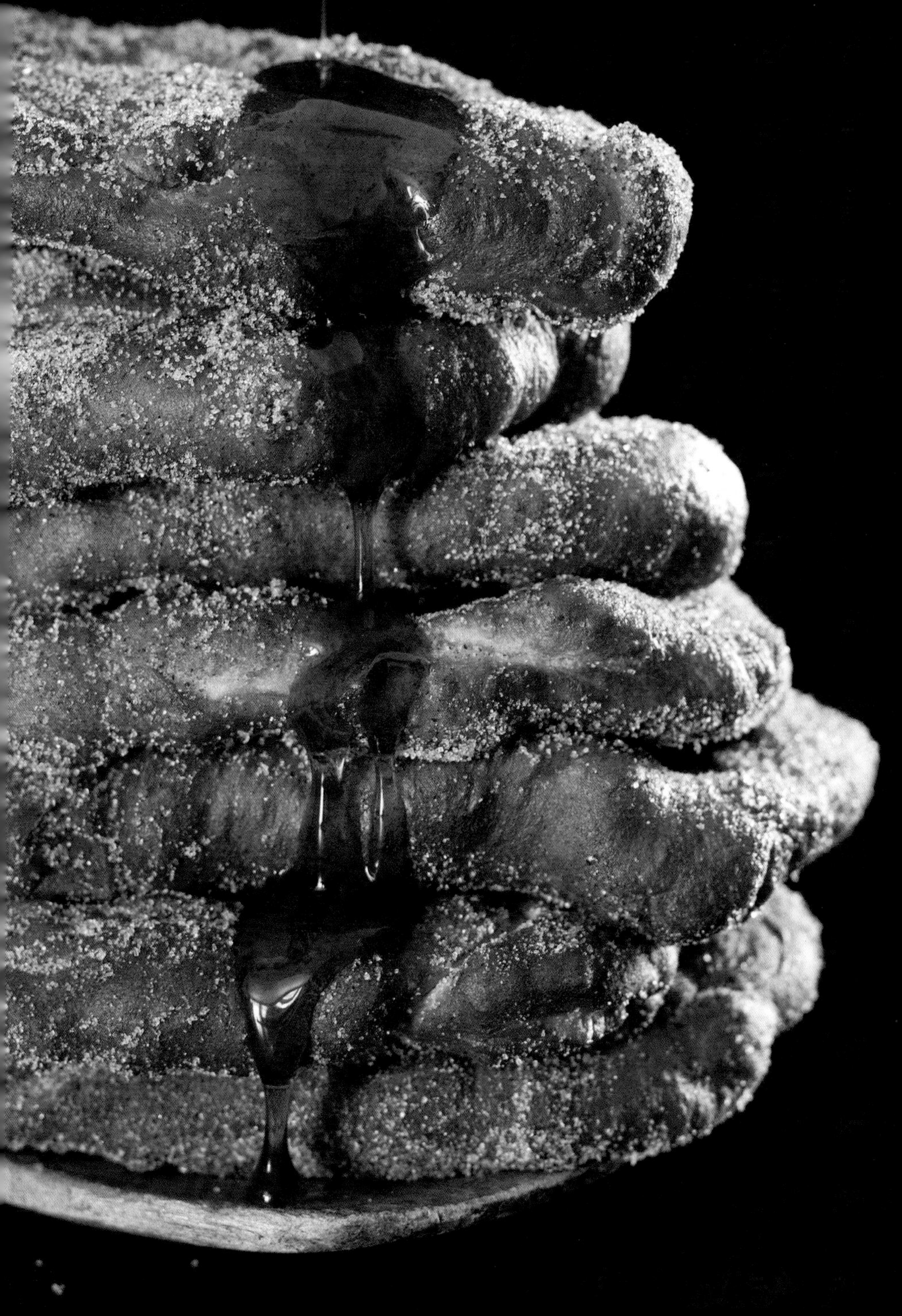

Tsoureki

Tsoureki is a braided Greek bread that is traditionally served at Easter. The three braids are meant to represent the Holy Trinity, and the red eggs represent the blood and suffering of Christ. Tsoureki has a soft, fluffy crumb, but what really sets it apart is the mahlep, a spice made from the seed of the Mahalep cherry native to the Middle East and the Mediterranean. Look for it, and the special vibrant red dye for the eggs, online or at your local ethnic grocery store. If you can't find mahlep, use vanilla extract instead. You won't get the same flavour, but the bread will still be delicious. Don't eat the eggs; they are meant as decoration and would likely be unpalatable after their time in the oven.

All-purpose flour	**1 1/2 cups**	**375 mL**
Sugar	**1 cup**	**250 mL**
1/4 oz. (7 g) packages active dry yeast	**2**	**2**
Warm whole milk	**1 cup**	**250 mL**
Large eggs, lightly beaten	**3**	**3**
All-purpose flour	**1 cup**	**250 mL**
Kosher salt	**2 tsp.**	**10 mL**
Unsalted butter, cut into pieces, softened	**1/2 cup**	**125 mL**
Orange juice	**2 tbsp.**	**30 mL**
Zest of 2 oranges		
Mahlep	**1 tbsp.**	**15 mL**
White bread flour	**3 cups**	**750 mL**
Large egg, lightly beaten	**1**	**1**
Red Easter eggs	**10**	**10**

Combine first amount of all-purpose flour, sugar and yeast in bowl of a stand mixer fitted with whisk attachment. Whisk on low to combine. Increase mixer speed to medium-low and gradually add milk, scraping down sides as necessary until combined. Cover bowl with plastic wrap and let stand for 30 minutes, until mixture is bubbling.

Change whisk attachment to dough hook. On medium speed, add first amount of egg in 3 additions. Add remaining all-purpose flour and salt, mixing until combined. Add butter, orange juice and zest and mahlep.

Gradually add 2 cups (500 mL) bread flour, scraping down sides of bowl if necessary. Add enough remaining bread flour to form a soft, slightly sticky dough that pulls away from sides. Mix dough on medium-high until smooth, about 8 minutes. Form dough into a ball and place in a greased bowl, turning to coat top. Cover with plastic wrap and let rise in oven with light on and door closed until doubled in size, about 1 1/2 hours.

(continued on next page)

(40 cm) strands. Take 3 strands and braid, pinching ends to seal. Repeat with remaining 3 strands. Place on baking sheets lined with parchment paper. Cover loosely with plastic wrap coated with cooking spray and let stand in oven with light on and door closed until doubled in size, about 1 1/2 hours.

Bake in 400°F (200°C) oven for 10 minutes. Remove from oven and push 5 eggs, larger side down, into centre of each loaf, spacing them evenly down length. Brush with remaining egg. Bake in 350°F (175°F) oven for 25 minutes, until loaves are golden and sound hollow when tapped on bottom. Transfer to wire rack to cool. Makes 2 loaves. Each loaf cuts into 16 slices.

1 slice: *140 Calories; 3.5 g Total Fat (1 g Mono, 0 g Poly, 2 g Sat); 10 mg Cholesterol; 24 g Carbohydrate (trace Fibre, 7 g Sugar); 4 g Protein; 170 mg Sodium*

Stollen

Stollen is a traditional German Christmas bread, filled with fruit, nuts and, often, marzipan. It dates back to the early 15th century in Dresden, Germany, though the original stollen was much different than the loaves baked today. Stollen was originally made with only flour, water and oil; butter and milk were banned during the Advent season. In the 17th century the Pope allowed butter and milk to be added to stollen, and it began to resemble the bread we are familiar with today. The characteristic shape of the loaf, shrouded in white icing sugar, is said to resemble the baby Jesus wrapped in swaddling clothes. Stollen pops up during the holiday season at German bakeries and delis throughout Canada, but it is more rewarding to make it yourself.

All-purpose flour	**1 1/2 cups**	**375 mL**
Sugar	**1/2 cup**	**125 mL**
Salt	**1 1/4 tsp.**	**6 mL**
1/4 oz. (7 g) packages of active dry yeast	**2**	**2**
Milk	**3/4 cup**	**175 mL**
Water	**1 cup**	**250 mL**
Margarine, softened	**2/3 cup**	**150 mL**
Eggs, room temperature	**3**	**3**
All-purpose flour	**4 1/2 cups**	**1.1 L**
Blanched almonds, chopped	**3/4 cup**	**175 mL**
Mixed candied fruits	**3/4 cup**	**175 mL**
Golden raisins	**1/3 cup**	**75 mL**
Icing sugar	**1 1/2 cups**	**375 mL**
Milk	**1 1/2 tsp.**	**7 mL**
Almond extract	**1/2 tsp.**	**2 mL**

In a large bowl, combine first amount of flour, sugar, salt and yeast.

Combine first amount of milk, water and margarine in a saucepan. Heat over low heat until liquids are hot to the touch. Gradually add to dry ingredients and beat for 2 minutes with an electric mixer at medium speed, or beat vigorously with a wooden spoon, scraping the bowl occasionally.

Add eggs and 1/2 cup (125 mL) flour. Beat at medium speed 1 minute, scraping the bowl. With a mixing spoon, stir in enough remaining flour to make a soft dough. Turn out on to a lightly floured surface. Knead dough until smooth and elastic, about 8 to 10 minutes.

Knead in blanched almonds, candied fruit and raisins. Place in a greased bowl, turning to grease top. Cover with a tea towel. Let stand in oven with light on and door closed until doubled in size, about 1 1/2 hours.

(continued on next page)

Punch dough down. Turn out onto a lightly floured surface. With a sharp knife cut dough into 3 equal pieces. Roll each piece into a 7 x 12 inch (18 x 30 cm) oval. Fold oval lengthwise in half. Press firmly only on the folded edge and don't tuck in the ends of the loaves. Place the stollen on greased baking sheets. Cover with tea towel and let stand in oven with light on and door closed until doubled in size, about 45 minutes. Bake in 350°F (175°C) oven for 20 to 25 minutes, or until hollow when tapped. Remove from pans and place on wire racks.

In a medium bowl, beat icing sugar, remaining milk and almond extract until mixture is smooth and has a creamy consistency. Spread over warm loaves. Makes 3 loaves. Cut each loaf into 12 slices.

1 slice: *180 Calories; 6 g Total Fat (2.5 g Mono, 1.5 g Poly, 1 g Sat); 20 mg Cholesterol; 28 g Carbohydrate (1 g Fibre, 2 g Sugar); 4 g Protein; 135 mg Sodium*

Panettone

Panettone originated in Milan but has gained popularity throughout Italy, with most regions of the country having their own versions. Panettone is traditional at Christmas, much like the ubiquitous fruitcake in Canada, but whereas fruitcake is often greeted with a lukewarm response, panettone in Italian families is a welcome treat. This bread can be a bit labour intensive, so where it was once made by local bakeries or in the home, most panettone now is commercially prepared. During the Christmas season, the huge, colourful boxes brighten the shelves of Italian centres across the land, here as in Italy. With this recipe, you can break free from store-bought panettone and bring a Christmas favourite back to the home kitchen, where it belongs. Feel free to add 1/2 cup (125 mL) cut mixed glazed fruit to the dough along with the raisins.

Large eggs	**3**	**3**
Very warm milk	**1/2 cup**	**125 mL**
Butter (or hard margarine), softened	**6 tbsp.**	**90 mL**
Warm water	**2/3 cup**	**150 mL**
Vanilla	**1 tsp.**	**5 mL**
All-purpose flour	**5 1/2 cups**	**1.4 L**
Sugar	**1/2 cup**	**125 mL**
1/4 oz. (7 g) instant yeast	**2**	**2**
Salt	**1 1/2 tsp.**	**7 mL**
Anise seeds (or 1 tsp., 5 mL, anise flavouring)	**1 tsp.**	**5 mL**
Light-coloured raisins	**3/4 cup**	**175 mL**
Medium-coloured raisins	**3/4 cup**	**175 mL**
Pine nuts	**1/2 cup**	**125 mL**
Grated lemon peel	**1 tsp.**	**5 mL**
Butter (or hard margarine), softened	**1 tbsp.**	**15 mL**

Beat eggs in a large bowl. Add milk, first amount of butter, water and vanilla. Stir until butter is melted.

Add 2 cups (500 mL) flour, sugar, yeast, salt and anise. Beat on low to moisten, then increase speed to medium and beat until smooth. Work in as much remaining flour as needed until dough pulls away from sides of bowl.

Stir in both types of raisins, pine nuts and peel. Knead dough 6 to 8 minutes. Place in a greased bowl, turning once to grease top. Cover with a tea towel. Let stand in oven with light on and door closed for about 1 1/2 hours until doubled in size. Punch dough down. Divide into 2 equal portions. Press each portion into a greased 9 inch (23 cm) springform pan.

(continued on next page)

Cover with greased waxed paper. Let stand in oven with light on and door closed for about 1 hour until doubled in size. Bake in 350°F (175°C) oven for about 45 minutes. Place on racks to cool. Brush warm tops with remaining butter. Makes 2 loaves. Each loaf cuts into 12 slices.

***1 slice:** 280 Calories; 6 g Total Fat (1.5 g Mono, 1.5 g Poly, 2.5 g Sat); 35 mg Cholesterol; 49 g Carbohydrate (2 g Fibre, 12 g Sugar); 7 g Protein; 160 mg Sodium*

Matzo

Out of respect for the trials of their ancestors, contemporary Jewish people forgo all leavened forms of bread during Passover and opt for matzo, the same bread their ancestors ate during Exodus in the Old Testament. To make this recipe kosher, substitute olive oil for the canola and bake the bread without letting it stand for 15 minutes. To get your matzo really thin, try running the dough through a pasta machine. Keep a close eye on it as it bakes because it burns easily. This bread also tastes good when the dough is sprayed or brushed lightly with water and sprinkled with salt before baking.

All-purpose flour	**4 1/2 cup**	**1.1 L**
Kosher salt	**1 tsp.**	**5 mL**
Canola oil	**2 tbsp.**	**30 mL**
Warm water	**3/4 cup**	**175 mL**

Heat a 10 x 15 inch (25 x 38 cm) baking sheet on bottom rack in 500°F (260°C) oven. In a large mixing bowl, combine flour, salt, oil and water, stirring until a dough forms. If dough is dry, add more water, a little at a time. Let dough stand for 15 minutes. Divide into 8 pieces. On a lightly floured surface, use a lightly floured rolling pin to roll each dough piece as thinly as possible into a 9 x 9 inch (23 x 23 cm) square. Cut each square into 9 equal squares and poke holes in surface of dough with a fork. Place on heated baking sheet and bake until surface looks golden and bubbly, 30 to 90 seconds. Use tongs to flip matzo pieces and bake until other side is golden, 15 to 30 seconds. Makes 72 squares.

***1 square:** 30 Calories; 0 g Total Fat (0 g Mono, 0 g Poly, 0 g Sat); 0 mg Cholesterol; 6 g Carbohydrate (0 g Fibre, 0 g Sugar); trace Protein; 30 mg Sodium*

Hot Cross Buns

These lightly spiced, fruit-filled rolls are best known as an English delicacy served at Easter celebrations. Their origins go back to medieval times, when the Saxons made buns marked with a cross for their spring celebration. Though breads marked with a cross go back much further, they did not contain the spices and dried fruit that hot cross buns are known for. For the Saxons, the sign of the cross may have symbolized the four seasons or the four quarters of the moon. When early Christians adopted hot cross buns for their own Good Friday services, the cross came to represent the cross on which Jesus was crucified. In England it is customary to have the cross on these buns made of dough that is baked into the bun, but in Canada, as in this recipe, it is often made of icing piped on top.

Milk, scalded and cooled to lukewarm	**2 cups**	**500 mL**
Sugar	**2 tsp.**	**10 mL**
Warm water	**1/2 cup**	**125 mL**
1/4 oz. (7 g) packages active dry yeast	**2**	**2**
All-purpose flour	**3 cups**	**750 mL**
Butter (or hard margarine), softened	**1/2 cup**	**125 mL**
Sugar	**3/4 cup**	**175 mL**
Large eggs	**2**	**2**
Salt	**1 tsp.**	**5 mL**
Ground cinnamon	**1 tsp.**	**5 mL**
Ground nutmeg	**1/8 tsp.**	**0.5 mL**
Ground cloves	**1/8 tsp.**	**0.5 mL**
Currants or raisins	**1 cup**	**250 mL**
All-purpose flour	**3 1/2 cups**	**875 mL**
Icing (confectioner's) sugar	**1 cup**	**250 mL**
Milk	**1 tbsp.**	**15 mL**
Vanilla extract	**1/4 tsp.**	**1 mL**
Butter (or hard margarine), softened	**2 tsp.**	**10 mL**

Pour first amount of milk into a large bowl. Set aside.

Stir first amount of sugar into warm water in a small bowl. Sprinkle yeast over top. Let stand 10 minutes. Stir to dissolve yeast. Stir into milk.

Beat in first amount of flour until very smooth. Cover with greased waxed paper and a tea towel. Let stand in oven with light on and door closed for about 50 minutes until bubbly and light.

(continued on next page)

Cream butter and remaining sugar in another bowl. Beat in eggs 1 at a time. Stir in next 5 ingredients. Add to flour mixture. Work in enough remaining flour so that dough pulls away from sides of bowl. Turn out onto a floured surface. Knead about 5 minutes until smooth and elastic. Place dough in a greased bowl, turning once to grease top. Cover with a tea towel. Let stand in oven with light on and door closed for about 1 hour until doubled in size. Punch dough down. Divide into 3 equal portions. Divide each portion into 12 pieces. Shape into buns. Arrange in 3 greased 8 x 8 inch (20 x 20 cm) pans. Cover with a tea towel. Let stand in oven with light on and door closed for about 1 hour until doubled in size. Cut with scissors or slash with knife or razor blade to make a cross on top 1/8 inch (3 mm) deep. Bake in 375°F (190°C) oven for 12 to 15 minutes. Turn out onto racks. Brush warm tops with remaining butter. Set aside to cool.

For the glaze, mix icing sugar, milk and vanilla together to make a barely pourable glaze. Drizzle or pipe over slashes in cooled buns. Makes 36 buns.

1 bun: *160 Calories; 3.5 g Total Fat (1 g Mono, 0 g Poly, 2 g Sat); 30 mg Cholesterol; 29 g Carbohydrate (trace Fibre, 11 g Sugar); 4 g Protein; 80 mg Sodium*

Why They Came...the Polish and Ukrainians

Concerned that Canada might lose territory to the Americans' doctrine of Manifest Destiny, in the late 19th century our government intensified its efforts to settle the West. Thanks to the gold rushes in BC, the west coast had a burgeoning population, but the huge area between there and Ontario was largely unsettled. The Dominion Lands Act of 1872 promised free land to any man willing to settle it, and the recently completed transcontinental railway was up and running, ready to whisk people to their new homesteads. Now all the government needed was agricultural settlers.

Historically, Canada had favoured immigrants from Britain, America and France, but Clifford Sifton, Minister of the Interior from 1896 to 1905, did not want those people. He feared they would simply move to urban centres rather than work the land. For his view of the prairies to become a reality, he needed peasants who would build homesteads and who knew how to work the land. For this, he turned to Eastern Europe. The Ukrainians were the largest group to settle in the prairies. The first wave of immigrants, 170,000 strong, lasted until the outbreak of World War I. These people were mostly farmers enticed by the offer of free land and the chance to escape the poverty plaguing their homeland. A second wave of Ukrainian immigrants arrived after the war ended, mostly people who were seeking political asylum. A third wave came at the end of World War II, made up of people who were displaced by war. Today, Canada has the third-largest population of Ukrainians in the world, after Ukraine and Russia. Communities in the prairies built by the early settlers are still going strong, preserving their language and culture.

The Ukrainians were not the only eastern Europeans who played a huge role in settling the prairies. Polish settlers also arrived in droves from the 1890s until World War I, when the government put the kibosh on immigration. Many of these people were also farmers, and they often set up their homesteads close to established Ukrainian settlements. When the war ended, Canada saw another wave of Polish immigration as expats sent for their families. Most of these people settled in urban areas, particularly in Edmonton, Calgary and Lethbridge. At the end of World War II, Canada opened its borders to survivors of concentration camps and those fleeing Soviet rule in Poland. Arrivals had to agree to work on farms in Alberta for two years, but could then move wherever they pleased. Today Edmonton has the largest Polish community in Alberta.

Kolach

Kolach is a braided or ring-shaped Ukrainian festive bread, featured at Christmas and other religious and family celebrations. The name "kolach" or "kalach" is derived from the Ukrainian word "kolo" or circle. The circle is an ancient symbol of eternity in many cultures. At Christmas, three kolach are stacked one atop the other and placed on a white cloth. A candle is inserted in the centre of the top loaf and burns throughout the evening meal. This rich, delicious bread is excellent fresh or toasted.

Sugar	**2 tsp.**	**10 mL**
Warm water	**1 cup**	**250 mL**
Active dry yeast	**1 tbsp.**	**15 mL**
Sugar	**1 cup**	**250 mL**
Water	**4 cups**	**1 L**
Butter (or hard margarine), melted	**3/4 cup**	**175 mL**
Salt	**1 tsp.**	**5 mL**
Large eggs, beaten	**5**	**5**
All-purpose flour, approximately	**12 1/2 cups**	**3.1 L**
Large egg	**1**	**1**
Water	**2 tbsp.**	**30 mL**

Stir in first amount of sugar in first amount of warm water in a small bowl. Sprinkle yeast over top. Let stand 10 minutes. Stir to dissolve yeast.

Stir remaining sugar into remaining water until dissolved. Stir in butter, salt, first amount of eggs and yeast mixture. Mix in 4 cups (1 L) flour and beat with an electric mixer until well blended. Mix in remaining flour with a wooden spoon. Dough should be fairly stiff so braids will hold their shape. Turn dough out onto a lightly floured surface. Knead dough until it is smooth and elastic, about 8 to 10 minutes. Cover and let stand in oven with light on and door closed until doubled in size, about 1 hour. Punch down and let stand again for 45 minutes. Divide dough into 3 portions. Divide each portion into 6 equal pieces. Roll 2 pieces into 24 inch long (30 cm) strips and place side by side on a baking tray. Braid dough. Repeat with remaining 4 pieces of dough. Place 1 braid into a well-greased 9 inch (23 cm) round cake pan, placing it around outside edge and pinching ends together. Place remaining braids side by side on work surface and braid, making a double braid. Form into a circle, trim ends and press dough together. Place double braid on top of and in centre of braid in pan. There will be a circular hole in middle of braids.

(continued on next page)

Repeat with remaining 2 portions of dough. Cover and let stand in oven with light on and door closed until doubled in size but not so long that braids lose their shape.

Combine remaining egg and water in a small bowl. Brush over loaves. Bake in 350°F (175°C) for 1 hour. Turn onto a wire rack to cool. Makes 3 loaves. Each loaf cuts into 14 pieces.

***1 slice:** 200 Calories; 4.5 g Total Fat (1 g Mono, 0.5 g Poly, 2.5 g Sat); 40 mg Cholesterol; 34 g Carbohydrate (1 g Fibre, 5 g Sugar); 5 g Protein; 65 mg Sodium*

Challah

Challah is a sweet egg bread baked for Jewish celebrations and holidays. It can take the form of a braided loaf or, when baked for the Jewish New year, a ring that symbolizes a year with no endings. Challah is made without dairy products so that it can be served with meat dishes and still be kosher. It has a soft white crumb with a dark brown crust. In the preparation of these loaves, Jewish women may take a small part of the dough and burn it in the oven as an offering to God. Sesame or poppy seeds are often sprinkled over top to represent God's providing manna in the desert during the Exodus.

1/4 oz. (7 g) package of active dry yeast	**1**	**1**
All-purpose flour	**2 cups**	**500 mL**
Sugar	**2 tbsp.**	**30 mL**
Salt	**1 1/2 tsp.**	**7 mL**
Hard margarine, softened	**1/3 cup**	**75 mL**
Hot water	**1 cup**	**250 mL**
Large egg	**1**	**1**
Saffron, pinch		
Large eggs, room temperature	**4**	**4**
All-purpose flour	**3 cups**	**750 mL**
Sugar	**2 tbsp.**	**30 mL**
Cold water	**1 tsp.**	**5 mL**

In a large bowl mix yeast, first amounts of flour and sugar, salt and butter. Gradually add hot water and beat with electric mixer at medium speed for 2 minutes, scraping bowl occasionally.

Separate 1 egg into yolk and white. Set aside. Add saffron, remaining eggs and egg white. The batter will be thick. Beat for 2 minutes at high speed. With a wooden spoon, mix in remaining flour, stirring until a soft dough forms that is no longer sticky. Turn dough out onto a lightly floured surface and knead about 8 minutes until dough is smooth and elastic. Place in a greased bowl and turn to coat top. Cover and let stand in oven with light on and door closed until doubled in size, about 1 hour. Punch dough down and knead out bubbles. Cut dough in half with a sharp knife. Cut each half into 3 pieces. Roll each piece into 12 inch (30 cm) strands. Lay 3 strands side by side and braid, starting from middle and working to one end. Pinch ends securely together, turn and braid other end. Repeat with remaining 3 strands.

(continued on next page)

Place braids on a baking sheet. Beat together remaining egg yolk, remaining sugar and cold water. Carefully brush braids with mixture. Let loaves stand, uncovered, in oven with light on and door closed for approximately 1 hour until doubled in size. Bake in 400°F (200°C) oven until a toothpick inserted in centre comes out clean and dry. Loaves will be shiny golden brown. Remove bread from oven and carefully remove from baking sheet to cool on wire rack. Handle loaves with care until they have cooled completely. Makes 2 loaves. Each loaf cuts into 18 slices.

1 slice: *90 Calories; 2 g Total Fat (0.5 g Mono, 0 g Poly, 1 g Sat); 10 mg Cholesterol; 15 g Carbohydrate (trace Fibre; 2 g Sugar); 2 g Protein; 100 mg Sodium*

Churros

Summer in Canada is festival season and with it comes a battalion of food trucks competing for your patronage. Nestled in amongst the kettle corn, lemonade, donair and ice cream trucks is the churros truck. Although they are a common street snack in Spain and Mexico, churros are not widely available in Canada and have become one of our favourite festival indulgences. If you just can't wait until summer, or don't want to brave the line-ups, this recipe has you covered. Churros are relatively simple to make at home, but make sure you use a star tip and do not have air bubbles in the dough as you push it out of the pastry bag or the churros can explode as they fry, spraying hot oil over everything in the vicinity.

Sugar	**1/4 cup**	**60 mL**
Ground cinnamon	**1/2 tsp.**	**2 mL**
Water	**1 cup**	**250 mL**
Sugar	**1 1/2 tbsp.**	**22 mL**
Salt	**1/2 tsp.**	**2 mL**
Vegetable oil	**1 tbsp.**	**15 mL**
All-purpose flour	**1 cup**	**250 mL**
Vegetable oil	**3 cups**	**750 mL**

In a paper bag or medium bowl, combine first amount of sugar and cinnamon. Set aside.

In a medium pot, heat water, remaining sugar, salt and first amount of oil on medium. Bring to a boil, then remove from heat. Stir in flour until mixture forms a ball.

Heat remaining oil in a deep skillet to 360°F (180°C). With a pastry bag or cookie press with a star tip, pipe 4 inch (10 cm) strips of dough onto a sheet of parchment paper. Using a spatula, transfer dough strips, 3 or 4 at a time, to hot oil. Do not cook too many strips at a time or the oil will cool and the churros will be chewy. Fry until golden, about 2 minutes per side, then transfer to a plate lined with paper towel to drain. Add hot churros to paper bag with cinnamon sugar mixture and shake until well coated. Makes 10 churros.

1 serving: *150 Calories; 9 g Total Fat (5 g Mono, 2.5 g Poly, 0.5 g Sat); 0 mg Cholesterol; 16 g Carbohydrate (0 g Fibre, 7 g Sugar); 1 g Protein; 115 mg Sodium*

INDEX